Letters to Mr. Malthus and A Catechism of Political Economy

J. B. Say

Translated by John Richter

LETTERS TO MR. MALTHUS, ON SEVERAL SUBJECTS OF POLITICAL ECONOMY, AND ON THE CAUSE OF THE STAGNATION OF COMMERCE. TO WHICH IS ADDED, A CATECHISM OF POLITICAL ECONOMY, OR FAMILIAR CONVERSATIONS ON THE MANNER IN WHICH WEALTH IS PRODUCED, DISTRIBUTED, AND CONSUMED IN SOCIETY,

J. B. SAY

TRANSLATED BY . JOHN RICHTER

1821

CONTENTS

PREFACE.

The science of Political Economy is at once one of the most important and interesting to mankind. It has in the course of a few years made great progress, and has attracted the attention and become the study of a considerable portion of the enlightened part of the public. Every attempt therefore to elucidate the subject of it will be kindly received, more particularly as a general knowledge of its principles cannot fail to produce incalculable advantages to the world.

Mr. Say was the first writer who attempted to raise Political Economy to the rank of the exact sciences:—how he has succeeded the public have the means of appreciating; posterity will decide. Until the appearance of the *Traité d'Economie Politique,* it had been limited to theories drawn from partial views of isolated facts and statistical histories, and from circumstances which it was always uncertain whether they had been fully observed or contemplated. No attempt was made to define the true nature of production, and to consider the thing in itself—to form just ideas on this subject; and, following them to their remotest consequences, to establish such a basis as should prove a true guide under every circumstance. Mr. Say had most clearly shewn that markets for commodities are created by and depend upon the production of commodities which can only be purchased by producers, or their representatives—not by unproductive consumers.

Mr. Malthus, in his *Principles of Political Economy,* and particularly in treating of the causes of the general stagnation of trade, has controverted this doctrine, together with some of the best established principles of the science. In these letters Mr. Say has entered the field of controversy—whether he will have added to his high reputation as a political economist, or Mr. Malthus will have disappointed the admirers of his *Essay on Population,* the public cannot fail to be benefitted by the discussion.

When the great truths of Political Economy shall become generally known—when men shall be convinced that each person will sell with greater facility the more others gain; that they can only gain by means of labour, capital, or land; that the greater the number of producers the greater the number of consumers; that unproductive consumers are mere representatives of others, and can only consume by means of what others produce; that all nations are interested in the prosperity of each other, and in facilitating the means of communication; that capital or land, and even labour, can only be productive while it is respected as property, and that the poor but industrious man is interested in the defence of the property of the rich, and in maintaining good order, because their subversion may deprive him of the means of subsistence:—when these truths shall be generally known, it will be almost impossible to stir up nations or bodies of men against each other. This science therefore is *eminently social,* and by teaching that no men can injure others without injuring themselves, and that the advantages gained by others are productive of advantages to themselves, will probably effect what a less interested doctrine has not yet accomplished.

J. R.

Cornwall Place,

1 *Jan.* 1821.

ADVERTISEMENT.

THE original of these letters came to my hands after translations of part of them had appeared in the New Monthly Magazine. *Expecting that they would afterwards be collected, I contented myself with comparing them for my own use; but this not being intended, and there appearing to be errors, and even contradictions, in several instances (perhaps inseparable from the fluency of the translation and mode of publication) as well as a want of that accuracy of expression necessary in scientific works, I have revised and continued the translation, and hope to have done a service to the public by presenting it in its present state. The quotations from English authors are given in the original words.*

J. R.

LETTER I.

Sir,

Every person who takes an interest in the new and interesting science of political economy, will certainly read the work with which you have lately enriched it. You are not one of those authors who claim the attention of the public, without having any information to communicate; and when the celebrity of the writer is added to the importance of the subject, when the question in debate is that momentous one to civilized society, namely, what are its means of existence and enjoyment? the curiosity of readers will undoubtedly be excited in an extraordinary degree.

I shall not attempt, Sir, to add my suffrage to that of the public, in pointing out the just and ingenious observations in your book; the undertaking would be too laborious. Nor shall I here discuss with you some points, to which, I think, you attach an importance which does not belong to them: I should be sorry to annoy either you or the public with dull and unprofitable disputes. But, I regret to say, that I find in your doctrines some fundamental principles which, if admitted under the imposing sanction of your authority, would occasion a retrograde movement in a science of which your extensive information and great talents are so well calculated to assist the progress.

In the first place my attention is fixed by the inquiry, so important to the present interests of society: What is the cause of the general glut of all the markets in the world, to which merchandize is incessantly carried to be sold at a loss? What is the reason that in the interior of every state, notwithstanding a desire of action adapted to all the developements of industry, there exists universally a difficulty of finding lucrative employments? And when the cause of this chronic disease is found, by what means is it to be remedied? On these questions depend the tranquillity and happiness of nations. A discussion therefore which tends to their illustration, I have not thought unworthy of your attention, or that of the enlightened public.

Since the time of Adam Smith, political economists have agreed that we do not in reality buy the objects we consume, with the money or circulating coin which we pay for them. We must in the first place have bought this money itself by the sale of productions of our own. To the proprietor of the mines whence this money is obtained, it is a production with which he purchases such commodities as he may have occasion for: to all those into whose hands this money afterwards passes, it is only the price of the productions which they have themselves created by means of their lands, capital, or industry. In selling these, they exchange first their productions for money; and they afterwards exchange this money for objects of consumption. It is then in strict reality with their productions that they make their purchases; it is impossible for them to buy any articles whatever to a greater amount than that which they have produced either by themselves, or by means of their capitals and lands.

From these premises I had drawn a conclusion which appeared to me evident, but which seems to have startled you. I had said, "As each of us can only purchase the productions of others with his own productions—as the value we can buy is equal to the value we can produce, the more men can produce, the more they will purchase." Thence follows the other conclusion, which you refuse to admit: "that if certain goods remain unsold, it is because other goods are not produced; and that it is production alone which opens markets to produce."

I am aware that this proposition has a paradoxical appearance, which creates prejudices against it; I know that common prejudices are more likely to support the opinions of those who maintain that there is too much produce, because every body is engaged in creating it: that instead of constantly producing, we ought to increase unproductive consumption, and devour our old capitals instead of accumulating new ones. This doctrine has indeed appearances on its side: it may be supported by arguments; and may interpret facts in its favour. But, Sir, when Copernicus and Galileo first taught that the sun (although it was daily seen to rise in the east, ascend majestically to the meridian, and decline at evening in the west) never moved from its station, they also had to contend with universal prejudice, the opinion of antiquity, the evidence of the senses: ought they to have renounced the demonstrations resulting from sound philosophy? I should wrong you, were I to doubt of your answer.

To proceed. When I advance that produce opens a vent for produce; that the means of industry, whatever they may be, when unshackled, always apply themselves to the objects most necessary to nations, and that these necessary objects create at once new populations and new enjoyments for those populations, all appearances are not against me. Let us only look back two hundred years, and suppose that a trader had carried a rich cargo to the places where New York and Philadelphia now stand; could he have sold it? Let us suppose even, that he had succeeded in founding there an agricultural or manufacturing establishment; could he have there sold a single article of his produce? No, undoubtedly. He must have consumed them himself. Why do we now see the contrary? Why is the merchandize carried to, or made at Philadelphia or New York, sure to be sold at the current price? It seems to me evident that it is because the cultivators, the traders, and now even the manufacturers of New York, Philadelphia, and the adjacent provinces, create, or send there, some productions, by means of which they purchase what is brought to them from other quarters.

Perhaps it will be said that "what is true with respect to a new state, may not be applicable to an old one: that there was in America room for new producers and new consumers; but in a country which already contains more producers than sufficient, additional consumers only are wanting." Permit me to answer, that the only true consumers are those who on their side produce, because they alone can buy the produce of others; and that unproductive consumers can buy nothing, unless by means of the value created by those who produce.

It is probable that so early as the time of Queen Elizabeth, when England was not half so populous as at present, it was already found

3

that the number of hands exceeded the quantity of employment: I desire no other proof of it than the poor law of that period, the consequences of which constitute one of the plagues of England. The principal object of it is to furnish work to the unfortunate who cannot obtain employment. They had no employment, in a country which has since been able to employ twice or thrice the number of workmen! How happens it, Sir, how happens it that, however unfortunate the situation of Great Britain may now be, much greater quantities of various kinds of goods are now sold there than in the time of Elizabeth? Whence can this arise, unless from the fact that the produce of that country is now greater? One man produces an article which he exchanges for another article produced by his neighbour. The means of subsistence having become greater, the population has increased, yet every one has been better provided for. It is the power of producing which makes the difference between a country and a desert; and a country is so much the more advanced, so much the more populous, and so much the better provisioned, as it increases in productions.

You will probably not object to this observation, which appears so obvious; but you deny the consequences which I draw from it. I have advanced that whenever there is a glut, a superabundance, of several sorts of merchandize, it is because other articles are not produced in sufficient quantities to be exchanged for the former; and if those who produce the latter could provide more of them, or of other goods, the former would then find the vent which they required: in short, that the superabundance of goods of one description arises from the deficiency of goods of another description. You, on the contrary, assert that there may be a superabundance of goods of all sorts at once; and you adduce several facts in favour of your opinion. M. Sismondi had already opposed my doctrine; and I am happy to quote here his strongest expressions, that I may not deprive you of any of your advantages, and that I may answer you and M. Sismondi at once.

"Europe," says that ingenious author, "has in every part arrived at the point of possessing industry and manufacturing power superior to its wants." He adds that the glut which results from it begins to affect the rest of the world: That, "In reading the commercial reports, the journals and accounts of travellers, we see on every side proofs of the superabundant production which exceeds consumption; of the manufacturing industry which is proportioned, not to the demand, but to the capital employed; of that mercantile activity which impels the merchants in crowds to every new market, and exposes them by turns to ruinous losses, in every branch of commerce from which they looked for profit. We have seen merchandize of every description, but above all that of England, the great manufacturing power, abounding in all the markets of Italy in a proportion so far exceeding the demand, that the merchants, in order to realize even a part of their capital, have been obliged to dispose of them at a loss of a fourth or a third, instead of obtaining any profit. The torrent of commerce repelled from Italy, flowed upon Germany, Russia, and Brazil, and soon found in those countries similar obstacles.

"The latest journals announce similar losses in new countries. In August 1818, they complained at the Cape of Good Hope that all the warehouses were filled with European merchandize, which, although offered at lower prices than in Europe, could not be sold. Similar complaints were made in June at Calcutta. Presently a strange phenomenon was seen, that of England sending her cotton goods, &c. to India, and consequently succeeding in working cheaper than the half-naked people of Hindostan, by reducing her workmen to a still more miserable existence! But the extraordinary direction thus given to commerce has not lasted long: even now, English manufactures are cheaper in the Indies than in England itself. In May, it it was found necessary to re-export from New Holland European merchandize which had been carried thither in excessive quantities. Buenos Ayres, New Granada, and Chili, are already sending back goods in a similar way.

"Mr. Fearon's journey in the United States, concluded only in the spring of 1818, presents the same spectacle in a manner still more striking. From one extremity of that vast and prosperous continent to the other, there is not even a village where the quantity of merchandize offered for sale is not infinitely superior to the means of the buyers, although the merchants labour to allure them by very long credits, and facilities of every kind for the payments, which they receive by instalments and in goods of every description.

"There are no facts which present themselves to us in so many places, and so many forms, as the disproportion between the means of consumption and the means of production—the inability of those who produce to abandon an employment when it becomes unprofitable,—and the certainty that their numbers are never reduced but by failures. How does it happen that philosophers refuse to perceive what meets the eyes of the vulgar in every direction?

"The error into which they have fallen arises entirely from the false principle that production is the same thing as revenue. Mr. Ricardo, following M. Say, thus repeats and confirms it. 'M. Say has proved in the most satisfactory manner,' he says, 'that there is no capital, however considerable, which cannot be employed, because the demand for production is limited only by production. No one produces any thing but with the intention of consuming or selling the thing produced; and nothing is ever sold but for the purpose of buying some other product, either of immediate utility, or calculated to contribute to future production. The producer therefore becomes the consumer of his own produce, or the purchaser and consumer of the produce of some other person.' Upon this principle," says M. Sismondi, "it becomes absolutely impossible to comprehend or explain the most established fact in the history of commerce—the glut of markets."*

I must remark to those to whom the facts which M. Sismondi justly regrets appear conclusive, that they are indeed conclusive, but that they are conclusive against himself. The quantity of English merchandize offered for sale in Italy and elsewhere is too great, because there is not sufficient Italian or other produce suitable to the English market. A country purchases only that for which it can pay; for, if it did not pay, people would soon tire of selling to it. But with what articles can the Italians pay the English? with oils, silks, and raisins; and besides those and a few other articles, if they would still acquire English produce, how are they to pay for them? With money!

But they must first acquire the money itself with which they are to pay for the English produce. You perceive, Sir, that to acquire foreign productions, a nation must, like an individual, have recourse to its own productions.

It is said that the English sell at a loss in those places which they inundate with their merchandize. This I believe to be true: they multiply the goods offered, which depreciates them; and they demand in return, as far as it is practicable, money only, which therefore becomes more rare and valuable. Being thus enhanced in value, money is given in smaller quantities in every exchange; and this is the reason why they are people obliged to sell at a loss. But suppose for an instant that the Italians possessed more capital; that they employed their lands and their industrious faculties to greater advantage; in short that they *produced* more; and suppose, at the same time, that the English laws, instead of having been modelled upon the absurd principles of the *balance* of trade, had admitted on moderate terms all that the Italians had been capable of furnishing in payment for the English productions; can you doubt that the English merchandize which incumbers the ports of Italy, and great quantities of other merchandize besides, would have been disposed of with facility?

Brazil, that vast country, so favoured by nature, might absorb a hundred times as much English merchandize as is now vainly sent there without finding a market; but it would first be requisite that Brazil should produce all that it is capable of producing; and how is that wretched country to attain that desirable object? All the efforts of the citizens are paralyzed by the government. If any branch of industry offers there the prospect of gain, it is instantly seized and stifled by the hand of power. Does any one find a precious stone, it is taken from him. Fine encouragement this to exert productive industry for the purpose of buying with its produce European merchandize!

The English government, on its part, by custom and import duties, refuses admission to the productions which the English might obtain by exchanges with foreigners; and even to the articles of food of which their manufacturers stand so much in need; and this because it is necessary that the English farmers should sell their corn at more than 80s. the quarter, to enable them to pay their excessive taxes. All these nations complain of a state of suffering into which they have been brought by their own fault; like diseased persons who bewail their maladies, and at the same time obstinately refuse to abandon the excesses which have caused them.

I know that it is not so easy to root up an oak as to pull up a weed; I know that old fences, however rotten, cannot be overthrown when they are supported by the heaps of filth which have accumulated beneath their shelter; I know that certain governments, corrupted and corrupting, stand in need of monopolies, and of custom duties, to pay for the votes of the honourable majorities which pretend to represent nations: I am not so unreasonable as to expect them to govern so entirely according to the general interest, as to be able to obtain the votes without paying for them; but, at the same time, why should I be astonished that such vicious systems have deplorable consequences?

You will, I presume, readily agree with me, as to the injuries which nations mutually sustain by their mutual jealousies, by the sordid interest or the inexperience of those who take upon themselves to be their organs; but you maintain, that even supposing they possessed more liberal institutions, the goods produced might exceed the wants of the consumers. Well, Sir, on this ground I am willing to rest my defence. Let us leave out of the question the war carried on between nations by means of their revenue officers; let us consider each nation in its relations with itself; and let us inquire, once for all, whether we have not the means of consuming what we have the means of producing.

"M. Say, Mr. Mill, and Mr. Ricardo," you say, "the principal authors of the new doctrines on profits, appear to me to have fallen into some fundamental errors on this subject. In the first place they have considered commodities as if they were so many mathematical figures, or arithmetical characters, the relations of which were to be compared, instead of articles of consumption, which must of course be referred to the numbers and wants of the consumers."*

I know not, Sir, at least so far as I am concerned, upon what foundation you have built this assertion. I have repeated, in a great variety of forms, this idea, that the *value* of things (the *only* quality by which they become wealth) is founded on their utility; on the aptitude which they possess to satisfy our wants. "The want which we have for any thing," I have said,* "depends on the physical and moral nature of man, on the climate which he inhabits, and the manners and laws of his country. He is subject to bodily wants, to mental and spiritual wants; some things he wants on his own account, others for his family; and others he requires as a member of society. A bear-skin and a rein-deer are to a Laplander objects of the first necessity; whilst the very names of them are wholly unknown to a *lazzarone* of Naples. The latter, for his part, can dispense with every other thing, if he is plentifully supplied with macaroni. In like manner, courts of justice, in Europe, are considered the strongest bonds of civil society; while the natives of America, the Arabs, and the Tartars, do very well without them - - -

"Of these wants, some are satisfied by the use which we make of certain things with which nature furnishes us gratuitously; as air, water, and the light of the sun. We may call these things *natural riches,* because the charges of their production is defrayed by nature herself. As she gives them without distinction to all, nobody is obliged to purchase them at the price of any sacrifice whatever. They have therefore no *exchangeable* value.

"Other wants can only be satisfied by the use which we make of certain things to which their utility could not have been given, without having subjected them to a modification, without having produced a change in their condition; without having, for this purpose, surmounted a difficulty of some kind. Such are the various goods which we can only obtain by the processes of agriculture, commerce, or the arts. These *only* have an *exchangeable* value. The reason of this is evident: they are, by the mere fact of their production, the result of an exchange, in which the producer has *given* his productive services, in order to *receive* this product. They cannot therefore be obtained from him, except by virtue of another exchange, in which some other product is given to him, which he may consider of equal value with his own.

"These things may therefore be called *social riches,* because no exchange can take place without a social relation, and because it is only in a state of society that the right of possessing exclusively what has been obtained by production or exchange, can be guaranteed."

I add, "Let us observe at the same time, that social riches are, as riches, the only ones which can become the object of scientific study; first, because they are the only ones which can be appreciated, or at least the only ones of which the appreciation is not arbitrary; and, secondly, because they alone are formed, distributed, and destroyed, according to laws which we are able to assign."

Is this to consider productions as *algebraic signs,* by abstracting them *from the number of consumers and the nature of their wants?* On the contrary, does not this doctrine establish that our wants alone induce us to make the sacrifices by means of which we obtain productions? These sacrifices are the price which we pay to procure them; you, like Smith, call these sacrifices by the name of *labour,* an inadequate expression, for they are partly composed of the use derived from land and capital. I call them *productive services.* They have everywhere a current price. When that price exceeds the value of the thing produced, the result is a disadvantageous exchange, in which the value consumed is greater than the value created. When a production has been created equal to the value of the services employed, those services are paid by the production, the value of which, distributed among the producers, forms their revenues. You see that the existence of these revenues depends upon the production having an *exchangeable* value, which it can only have in consequence of the want which there is for such production in the actual state of society. Therefore I do not abstract this want, or give it an arbitrary appreciation; I take it for what it is, for what the consumers make it to be. I could have cited, had it been necessary, the whole of my third book, which details the different modes, motives, and results of consumption, but I will not trifle with your time and attention:—let us proceed.

You say,* "It is by no means true, as a matter of fact, that commodities are always exchanged for commodities. The great mass of commodities is exchanged directly for labour, either productive or unproductive; and it is quite obvious that this mass of commodities, compared with the labour with which it is to be exchanged, may fall in value from a glut just as any one commodity falls in value, from an excess of supply, compared either with labour or money." Permit me to remark, in the first place, that I never said, commodities are always exchanged for commodities; but that *productions can only be purchased by productions.*

Secondly, that even those who admit this expression of *commodities* might answer you, that when commodities are given in exchange for labour, these commodities are in reality given in exchange for other commodities, that is to say, for those which result from the labour which has been purchased. But this answer is insufficient for those who embrace in a more extended and complete view, the phenomenon of the production of our riches. Allow me to place it before your eyes in a striking form. The public, which is to judge between us, will, I think, be thus materially assisted in appreciating your objections and my answers.

To obtain a better view of the operations of industry, capital, and land, in the work of production, I personify them: and I discover that all these personages sell their services, which I call *productive services,* to a speculator, who may be either a trader, a manufacturer, or a farmer. This speculator having purchased the services of a landed estate, by paying a rent to the proprietor; the services of a capital, by paying interest to the capitalist; and the industrious services of workmen, factors, agents of whatever description, by the payment of salaries;—consumes all these productive services, annihilates them; and out of this consumption comes a production which has a value.

The value of this production, provided it be equal to the costs of production, that is to say, to the sum necessarily advanced for all the productive services, suffices to pay the profits of all those who have concurred directly or indirectly in this production. The profit of the speculator on whose account this operation has been effected, deducting the interest of the capital which he may have employed, represents the remuneration for his time and talents; that is to say, his own productive services employed in his own behalf. If his abilities be great, and his calculations well made, his profit will be considerable. If instead of talent he evinces inexperience in his affairs, he may gain nothing; he may very probably be a loser. All the risks attach to the speculator; but on the other hand he takes the advantage of all the favourable chances.

Every production which we see, or which our imagination conceives, is formed by operations which resolve themselves, without exception, into those which I have described, but combined in an infinity of different manners. What some speculators are doing for one sort of production, others perform for another sort. Now, it is the exchanging of these articles one for another which constitutes a market for each. The greater or less want that exists for one of these productions, compared with the others, determines the greater or less price which is given to obtain it; that is to say, the greater or less quantity of any other production. Money is in these transactions only a transient agent, which, when once the exchange is completed, is no farther concerned in it, and flies to effect other exchanges.

It is with the rent, interest, and wages, which form the profits resulting from this production, that the producers buy the objects of their consumption. These producers are at the same time consumers; and the nature of their wants, influencing in different degrees the demand for different kinds of produce, is always favourable, where liberty exists, to the most necessary kind of production; because that, being the most in demand, affords to those who produce it the greatest profits.

I said that in order to see how industry, capital, and land respectively act in productive operations, I personified them, and observed them in the services they rendered. But this is not a gratuitous fiction; it is a fact. Industry is represented by the *industrious* of all classes; capital, by *capitalists;* land by its *proprietors.* These are the three orders of persons who sell the productive services of the instrument they possess, and stipulate the remuneration for its employment. My expressions may perhaps be objected to; but it will then be incumbent on those who find fault with them, to propose better, for it is impossible to deny that this is the course of the transactions. I have stated the fact. The manner of the painter may be criticized, but the facts represented defy contradiction; there they are, and they will defend themselves.

To return to your assertion. You say, Sir, that many commodities are purchased with labour; and I go farther than you: I say, they are all purchased with *labour,* extending that expression to the services rendered by capital and land.* I say that they cannot be purchased by any other means; that the value and utility of things in all cases are produced by such services; and that the alternative is thus presented to us: either to consume ourselves the utility, and consequently the value which we have produced, or to employ it in the purchase of the utility and value produced by others; that in both cases we purchase commodities with productive services, and that the more productive services we carry to market, the more we can buy in return.

You assert that there are no *immaterial productions.* Why, Sir, originally there were no other. A field, for instance, furnishes towards production only its service, which is an immaterial product. It serves as a crucible into which you put a mineral, and extract metal and dross. Is there any part of the crucible in these products? No; the crucible serves for a new productive operation. Is there any portion of the field in the harvest which is obtained from it? I answer likewise, No; for if land were thus gradually consumed, it would cease to exist in a few years: the land only returns what is put into it; but returns it after an elaboration, which I call the *productive service* of the field. Possibly some people may quibble on the word. I do not apprehend any quibbles that may be attempted as to the thing, because that is undeniable, and wherever political economy shall be studied, will be acknowledged as the fact, whatever name people may think proper to give it.

The service rendered by capital in any undertaking whatever, commercial, agricultural, or manufactoral, is likewise an *immaterial product*. He who consumes a capital unproductively destroys the capital itself; he who consumes it reproductively, consumes the material capital, and also the service of that capital, which is an *immaterialproduct*. When a dyer puts indigo, to the value of a thousand francs, into his copper, he *consumes* material produce worth a thousand francs; and, besides, he consumes the hire of this capital, its interest. The dye which he obtains, returns to him the value of the material capital employed, and also the value of the *immaterial* service of the same capital. The service of the workman is likewise an *immaterial* product. The workman comes out of the manufactory at night with the ten fingers which he carried into it in the morning. He has left nothing material in the workshop. It is then an immaterial service which he has furnished towards the productive operation. This service is the daily or annual produce of a fund or estate which I call his *industrious faculties,* and which compose his riches: miserable riches! particularly in England; - - and I know the reason.

All these are *immaterial productions,* which, call them as you please, will still be immaterial productions, exchangeable mutually one with another, exchangeable for material productions; and which, in all exchanges, will still seek their market-price, founded, like every market-price in the world, upon the proportion between the supply and demand.

These services, of industry, capital, and land, which are products independent of all matter, form all our revenues, much as we are - - - - What! all our revenues immaterial!!! Yes, Sir, All: otherwise the mass of matter which composes the globe would increase every year; it must happen so, for we should every year have new material revenues. We neither create nor destroy a single atom. All that we do is to change the combinations of things; and all that we add is immaterial. It is value; and it is this value which is immaterial also, that we daily, annually consume, and upon which we live; for consumption is a change of form given to matter, or, if you prefer the expression, a derangement, as production is an arrangement of form.

If you find a paradoxical appearance in these propositions, examine the things which they express, and I have no doubt they will appear very simple and reasonable.

Without this analysis, I defy you to explain the whole of the facts; for instance, how the same capital is twice consumed: *productively,* by a speculator, and *unproductively,* by his workman. By means of the foregoing analysis, it may be seen how the workman brings to market his labour, the fruits of his ability; he sells it to the master, carries home with him his wages, which forms his revenue, and consumes it unproductively. But the master, who has bought the labour of the workman with a part of his capital consumes it reproductively, as the dyer consumes reproductively the indigo thrown into his copper. These values having been consumed reproductively, reappear in the production which comes out of the hands of the master. It is not the capital of the master which forms [Editor: illegible word] revenue of the workman, as M. *Sismondi* pretends. The capital of the master is consumed in the workshops. and not in the maintenance of the workman. The value consumed by the latter has another source; it is the produce of his industrious faculties. The master devotes to the purchase of the workman's labour a part of his capital. Having purchased it, he consumes it; and the workman consumes, on his part, the value which he has obtained in exchange for his labour. Wherever there is exchange, there are two values created and bartered one for the other; and wherever two values are created, there must be, and there are, in effect, two consumptions.*

It is the same with the *productive service* rendered by capital. The capitalist who lends, sells the service, the labour of his instrument; the daily or annual hire, which a speculator pays him for it, is called *interest.* The terms of the exchange are, on one side, the service of the capital, on the other, the interest. The speculator, while he consumes reproductively the capital, also consumes reproductively the *service* of the capital. The lender, on the other hand, who has sold the service of the capital, consumes the interest unproductively, which is a material value given in exchange for the immaterial service of the capital. Ought we to wonder that there should be a double consumption, that of the speculator to make his production, and that of the capitalist to satisfy his wants, since there are the two terms of an exchange, two values drawn from two different funds, bartered for each other, and both capable of consumption?

You say, Sir, that the distinction between productive and unproductive labour is the corner-stone of Adam Smith's work; that to recognise as productive, labours which are not fixed in any material object (as I do) is to overturn that work from top to bottom.* No, Sir; that is not the corner-stone of Smith's work; for when that stone is removed, the edifice, although imperfect, remains as solid as before. What will eternally sustain that excellent book is, that it proclaims in every page that the *exchangeable value* of things is the foundation of all riches. From the publication of that important truth, political economy became a positive science; for the market-price of every thing is a determinate quantity of which the elements may be analysed, the causes assigned, the relations studied, and the consequences foreseen. Permit me, Sir, to say that to separate this essential character from the definition of wealth, is to plunge the science again into the depths of obscurity—to drive it back.

Instead of weakening the authority of the celebrated *Inquiry into the Wealth of Nations,* I support it in the most essential part; but at the same time I think Adam Smith has forgotten some real exchangeable values, in omitting those which are attached to such productive services as leave no trace because they are totally consumed; I think that he has likewise misunderstood services unquestionably real, which even leave their traces in material produce; such are the services of capital, consumed independently of the consumption of the capital itself; I think that he fell into infinite obscurities through omitting to distinguish, in the course of production, the consumption of the industrious services of a speculator from the services of his capital; a distinction which nevertheless is so real, that there is scarcely any commercial association whose regulations do not contain clauses relative to it.

I revere *Adam Smith*—he is my master. When I took the first steps in political economy, and when still tottering I was pushed by the advocates of the balance of commerce on the one side, and the advocates of net produce on the other, I stumbled at every move—he shewed me the true path. Supported by his *Wealth of Nations,* which shews at the same time his own intellectual wealth, I learned to go alone. Now I have ceased to belong to any school, and I shall escape the sort of ridicule which attached to the reverend father Jesuits who translated the Elements of Newton with annotations. They were sensible that physical laws would not square very well with those of Loyola; they therefore took care to inform the public by an advertisement, that, although they had apparently demonstrated the motion of the earth to complete the theory of celestial physics, they nevertheless bowed with submissive acquiescence to the decrees of the Pope, who did not acknowledge this motion. I submit only to the decrees of eternal reason, and am not afraid to declare it: Adam Smith has not embraced all the phenomena of the production and consumption of wealth; but he has done so much that we ought to feel the deepest gratitude for his exertions. The most vague and obscure of all the sciences, will, thanks to his researches, soon become the most precise, and leave fewer facts unexplained than any of the others.

Let us then figure to ourselves the producers (by which name I mean as well the possessors of capital and of land, as the possessors of industrious faculties); let us imagine them pressing forwards with emulation to offer their productive services, or the *utility* derived from them, (an immaterial quality). This utility is their production. Sometimes it is fixed in a material object, which passes with the immaterial produce, but which in itself is of no importance, is nothing in political economy; for matter deprived of value is not wealth. Sometimes it passes, sold by one and bought by another, without being fixed in any substance—as the advice of the physician, that of the lawyer, the service of the soldier, and of the public functionary. All these exchange the utility which they produce for that which is produced by others; and in as many of these exchanges as are abandoned to free competition, according as the utility offered by *Paul* is more or less in demand than the utility offered by *James,* it is sold more or less dear, that is to say, it obtains in exchange, more or less of the utility produced by the latter. It is in this sense that we should understand the influence of *demand* and *supply*.

This, Sir, is not a doctrine retrospectively made for the occasion; it is delivered in several parts of my *Traité d'Economic Politique;** and by means of my *Epitome,* its concordance with all the other principles of the science, and with all the facts which form its basis is firmly established. It is already professed in several parts of Europe; but I ardently wish to see you convinced of its truth, and that you may think it worthy of the support of that chair which you fill with so much credit.

After these necessary explanations, you will not accuse me of vain subleties, if I rely on the laws which I have shewn to be founded on the nature of things, and the facts which flow from that source.

Commodities, you say, are not exchanged for commodities only; they are also exchanged for labour. If this labour be a product which some sell and others buy and consume, I shall find little difficulty in calling it a *commodity,* and you will find little in assimilating other commodities to this, for they are also productions. If you will apply to each of them indiscriminately the generic name of production, you will probably agree with me that productions can only be purchased with productions.

Notes

[*] Nouveaux Principes d'Economie Politique, de Sismondi, tom. i. p. 337.

[*] Malthus's "Principles of Political Economy," p. 354.

[*] Traité d'Economie Politique, &c. 4e édition, tom. ii. p. 5. See also, Catechism of Political Economy.

[*] Malthus's Principles of Political Economy, p. 153.

[*] The English authors are often obscure through their confounding, like Smith, under the denomination of *labour*, the services rendered by men, by capital, and by land.

[*] A domestic produces personal services which are wholly consumed unproductively by his master, as soon as produced. The service of the public functionary is in like manner wholly consumed by the public, as fast as it is produced. That is the reason why these different services contribute nothing to the augmentation of riches. The consumer enjoys these services, but cannot accumulate them. This is explained in detail in my "Traité d'Economie Politique," 4e edition, tom. i. p. 124; and also in my Catechism of Political Economy. After that it is difficult to conceive how M. Malthus could print (p. 35.), "I am hardly aware how the causes of the increasing riches and prosperity of Europe since the feudal times could be traced, if we were to consider personal services as equally productive of wealth with the labour of merchants and manufacturers." It is with these services as with the labour of the gardener, who has cultivated salads or strawberries. The wealth of Europe certainly does not arise from the strawberries which have been produced, because they must, like personal services, have been consumed unproductively as fast as they ripened, although less quickly than personal services.

I have instanced strawberries as a very perishable product; but it is not the durability of a production which particularly facilitates accumulation. It is because it is consumed in a manner adapted to reproduce its value in another object. For whether durable or not, every product is devoted to consumption, and answers no purpose whatever except by its consumption; this purpose is either to satisfy a want, or to reproduce a new value. When people undertake to write on political economy, they should dismiss from their minds the notion that durable produce accumulates better than what is perishable.

[*] Malthus on Political Economy, p. 37.

[*] 4e edit. L. i. ch. 15; L. ii. ch. 1, 2, 3, & 5; and also the *Epitome* at the end, at the words, Productive Services, Charges of Production, Income, Utility, Value.

LETTER II.

Sir,

I think I have proved in my first letter that productions can only be purchased with productions: I do not therefore yet see any reason to abandon the doctrine, that it is production which opens a market to production. I have indeed considered as productions all the services arising from our personal capacities, from our capitals, and our lands; which has obliged me to sketch anew, and in other terms, the doctrine of production, which *Smith* evidently did not comprehend, and has not completely described.

But on reading again the third section of your 7th chapter (p. 351) I feel that there is still a point on which you will not agree with me. You will probably grant that productions can only be bought with productions; but you will persist in maintaining that people may create a quantity of produce in the whole exceeding their wants, and that consequently part of this produce can not be used; that there may be a superabundance and glut of all commodities at once. In order to present your objection in its full force, I shall transform it into a sensible image, by saying: Mr. Malthus will readily allow that 100 sacks of corn will buy 100 pieces of stuff, in a society which has occasion for those quantities of stuff and corn for its raiment and food; but if the same society should happen to produce 200 sacks of corn and 200 pieces of stuff, although these two commodities may still be exchangeable for each other, he will maintain that a part of each of them will no longer find purchasers. It is therefore necessary for me to prove, first, that whatever may be the quantity produced, and the consequent depression of price, a quantity produced of one species always suffices to enable those who have produced it to acquire the quantity produced of another species; and after proving that the possibility of acquiring exists, I shall endeavour to shew how the superabundance of productions creates a demand for it, for the purpose of consumption.

The farmer who produces corn, after having purchased the productive services of the land and capital which he employs, as well as those of his labourers, and added to these services that of his own personal labour, has consumed all those values to convert them into sacks of corn; let us suppose that each sack stands him in thirty shillings, including the value of his own labour, that is to say, his profit. On the other hand the manufacturer who produces stuffs of linen, woollen, or cotton, after having consumed in like manner the services of his capital, those of his workmen and himself, has produced stuffs which stand him also in thirty shillings the piece. If I may be permitted to jump at once to the main point of the inquiry, I will premise that this manufacturer of stuffs represents in my mind the producers of all manufactured produce, and this grower of corn the producers of all provisions and raw materials. The question is, whether their two articles of produce, to whatever quantities they may be multiplied, and whatever depression of price may result from that multiplication, can be wholly purchased by the producers, who are also at the same time the consumers; and how wants arise always in proportion to the quantity of productions.

We must first inquire into the course of things upon the hypothesis of a perfect liberty, permitting the indefinite multiplication of all productions; and we will afterwards examine the obstacles which the nature of things, or the imperfection of society opposes to this unrestricted freedom of production; but you will remark that the hypothesis of unrestricted production is more favourable to your cause, because it is much more difficult to dispose of unlimited produce than of that which is restricted; and that the hypothesis of production restricted sometimes by one cause and sometimes by another, is more favourable to mine, which supports the doctrine that these restrictions are the very causes which, by restraining certain productions, impede the purchases which might be made of the only productions which can be indefinitely multiplied.

Upon the hypothesis, then, of perfect liberty, suppose the grower brings to market a sack of corn, which including his profit, comes to thirty shillings, and the manufacturer brings a piece of stuff which comes to the same price, and consequently these productions will be exchangeable at par.* Of these two dealers, if one have gained more than his costs of production, he will draw into his line of business a part of the persons occupied in the production of the other article, until in both parts productive services shall be equally well paid: this is an effect generally allowed.

Here we ought to observe, that upon this supposition, the producers of the piece of stuff have *altogether* gained wherewith to repurchase that entire piece, or to buy any other product of equal value. If, for instance, it amounts to thirty shillings, including all expenses, as well as the profit of the manufacturer at the current rate, this sum is distributed amongst all the persons concerned in the production of the piece of stuff; but in unequal shares, according to the nature and amount of the services which they have rendered in the operation of its production. If the piece contain ten yards, he who has received six shillings can buy two yards of it; he who has received eighteen pence can only buy half a yard: but all of them together can certainly buy the whole piece. But if instead of the stuff, they wish to buy the corn, they are able, together, to purchase the whole quantity, since its value is the same with that of the stuff; so each of them can purchase, according to their respective occasions, either a part of the piece of stuff, or an equivalent portion of the sack of corn. He who has received for his services in either of these productions six shillings, may use three shillings in the purchase of a tenth part of the piece of stuff, and three shillings in buying a tenth of the corn; in all cases it is clear that all the producers possess *collectively* the means of acquiring the whole of the productions.

Now, Sir, come your objections. If commodities increase, or wants diminish, you say, commodities will fall to a price too low to pay the labour requisite for their production.*

In proceeding to answer this objection, I wish to premise, that if I consent to employ your word *labour*, which, according to the explanation given in my former letter, is incomplete, I shall comprehend under that denomination, not only the productive services of the workman and his master, but the productive services rendered by capital and land; services which have their price, as well as personal labour, and a price so strictly real, that the capitalist and the landholder live upon it.

This point being understood, I answer you in the first place, that the depression of the price of productions, does not prevent the producers from purchasing the labour which has created them, or any other equivalent labour. In our hypothesis, the grower of corn will, by an improved process, produce a double quantity of corn, and the manufacturer a double quantity of stuffs; and the corn and stuffs will fall to half their prices. What then? The producers of corn will receive for the same services as before, two sacks worth only what one sack was before worth, and the producers of stuffs will have two pieces together of the same value, as one piece had formerly been: In the exchange called *production,* the same services will have respectively obtained a double quantity of produce; but these double quantities may be acquired by each other as before, and as easily as ever; so that without a greater expense in productive services, a nation in which this productive faculty should be thus developed, would have double the quantity of commodities for consumption, in corn or stuffs, or even in other articles; as we have agreed to represent by corn and stuffs, all things of which men stand in need for their support and accommodation. Productions in such an exchange are valued against productive services; now as in every exchange, the value of one of the terms is greater in proportion to the greater quantity of the other which it obtains, it follows that productive services are increased in value in proportion as productions are increased in quantity, and diminished in price.* This is the reason why the reduction of the price of productions, by increasing the value of the productive funds of a nation and of the income derived therefrom, augments the national wealth. I think this demonstration, which may be seen at length in my *Traité d'Economic Politique,* 4th edition, book ii. ch. 3, has done some service to science, by elucidating what previously had been felt, but not explained; that is to say, that although wealth is an exchangeable value, the general wealth is increased by the low price of commodities and productions of all sorts.†

Probably it never happened that the productive power of labour was suddenly doubled; and for all productions at once; but a gradual augmentation with respect to many articles, and in various proportions, has undoubtedly occurred. Among the antients, a scarlet mantle of equal fineness and size, solidity of texture and beauty of colour, to one of ours, cost unquestionably more than double the price it would cost amongst us; and I have no doubt that the corn, paid in labour, fell in value at least half at the unknown period of the invention of the plough. These articles, costing less labour, were, in consequence of the competition, given for what they cost, without any one being a loser; while all gained in their revenues by the event.

But to return to the first part of your objection: *The growers of corn and makers of stuffs will then produce more corn and stuffs than they can consume.* Ah! my good Sir, after having proved that notwithstanding a fall of one half in the value of productions, the same labour may purchase the *whole* of them, and thereby procure an increase of as much again in the necessaries and luxuries of life, can it be necessary for me to prove to the justly celebrated author of the *Essay on Population,* that whatever is produced will find consumers, and that among the enjoyments procured by the quantity of productions which men can command, they do not place in the inferior ranks the comforts of a home, and the increase and preservation of their children? After having written three justly admired volumes, to prove that population always rises to the level of the means of subsistence, can you possibly have admitted the supposition *of a great augmentation of produce, with a stationary number of consumers, and wants diminished by parsimony?* (p. 355.)

Either the author of the "*Essay on Population,*" or the author of "*Principles of Political Economy,*" must be in the wrong. But every thing convinces us that it is not the former who is mistaken. Experience, as well as reasoning, demonstrates that a production, *an article necessary or agreeable* to man, is only rejected when people have not the means of paying for it. These means of purchasing are precisely those which establish the demand for a production, and give it a price. Not to want an useful thing is not to be able to pay for it. And what occasions this inability to pay for it? The being deprived of that which constitutes wealth: the being deprived of industry, land, or capital.

As soon as men are provided with the means of producing, they appropriate their productions to their wants; for production itself is an exchange, in which we *offer* (or *supply*) productive means, and *demand* in return the thing of which we feel the greatest *want*. To create a thing which no one wanted, would be to create a thing without value: it would not be to produce. But the moment it has a value, its producer may exchange it for other commodities which he may wish to procure.

This faculty of exchange, peculiar to man alone, among all the animals, adapts all productions to all wants; and permits him to depend, for his subsistence, not upon the kind of his production (for he can exchange it when he pleases, if it has value,) but upon its value.

The difficulty, you will say, is to create productions which shall be worth the costs of production. This I well know; and, in my next letter, you will find what I think on the subject. But upon the hypothesis which we have already supposed, of the freedom of industry, permit me to point out that the only difficulty we find in creating productions worth the costs of production, arises from the high demands of the vendors of productive services. Now the high price of productive services denotes that what is required exists; namely, that there are employments, the productions of which suffice to repay the costs of production.

You charge those who entertain the same opinions with me, with "not taking into consideration the influence of so general and important a principle in human nature, as indolence, or the love of case." (p. 358.) You suppose the case that men, after having produced the means of satisfying their primary and most urgent wants, would prefer doing nothing more; the love of repose overbalancing in their minds the desire of enjoyment. This supposition is all in my favour. What do I say? That things are only sold to those who produce. Why are objects of luxury not sold to a farmer who chooses to lead a homely life? Because he prefers ease to the trouble of producing the means of purchasing objects of luxury. Whatever be the cause which limits production, whether the want of capital or of population, of diligence or liberty, the effect is, in my opinion, the same; the productions which are offered on one side are not sold, because sufficient commodities are not produced on the other.

You consider the indolence which refuses to produce as directly impeding the sale of productions, and I entirely agree with you on that point. But then, how can you look on the indolence of those whom you call *unproductive consumers,* as favourable to such sales. (c. vii. sect. 9.) "It is absolutely necessary," you say, (page 463,) "that a country with great powers of production should possess a body of unproductive consumers." How comes it that the indolence that refuses to produce is prejudicial to the markets in the former case, and favourable to them in the latter?

The fact is, this indolence is injurious to them in both cases. Whom do you designate by this numerous body of unproductive consumers, so necessary, according to you, to the producers? Is it the proprietors of lands and capitals? Undoubtedly they do not directly produce, but their instrument (their property) does it for them. They consume the value to the creation of which their lands and capitals have contributed. They therefore assist in production, and can only make purchases in consequence of this assistance. If they also contribute their personal services, and join to their profits as capitalists and landholders other profits as labourers, they can, by thus producing more, consume more; but it is not in their non-productive capacity that they increase the markets for the sale of productions.

Do you allude to public functionaries, the military, and fundholders? Still it is not on account of their non-productive quality that they increase the demand for produce. I am far from disputing the legitimacy of the emoluments which they receive; but I cannot believe that those who are taxed would be very much embarrassed by their money, even if these receivers of contributions did not come to their assistance: either their wants would be more amply satisfied, or they would employ this same money in a reproductive manner. In either case the money would be expended, and would promote the sale of some productions of equal value to what is now bought by those whom you call *unproductive consumers*. Confess then, Sir, that it is not through the unproductive consumers that sales are promoted, but by the productions of those who provide the means for their expenditure; and that even should all the unproductive consumers vanish, which heaven forbid, there would not be a pennyworth the less sold.

Nor do I know on what better foundation you decide (page 356,) that production cannot continue if the value of the commodities pays for but little labour beyond what they cost. It is by no means necessary to the continuance of production that a commodity should be worth more than the costs of its production. When an undertaking is begun with a capital of a hundred thousand pounds, it is sufficient to enable the proprietors to re-commence their operations, that the production which results from it should be worth a hundred thousand pounds. Where then, say you, are the profits of the producers? The whole capital has served to pay them;* and it is the price which it has paid to them which has formed the incomes of all the producers. If the produce which has been obtained be worth only one hundred thousand pounds, there is the capital reestablished, and all the producers are paid.*

I do not hesitate to strengthen your objection, by expressing it thus:—"Though each commodity may have cost the same quantity of labour and capital in its production, and they may be exactly equivalent to each other, yet they may both be so abundant, that they will not purchase more labour than they have cost. In this case, can production go on? Unquestionably not."

And why not, I pray? Why could not farmers and manufacturers, who had produced together to the amount of sixty shillings in corn and stuffs, and would, as I have demonstrated, be able to purchase the whole of those commodities, sufficient for their wants—why could they not recommence their operations after making such purchases, and consuming the articles bought? They would have the same lands, the same capitals, the same industry as before; they would be precisely where they began; and they would have lived and been supported by their incomes, by the sale of their productive services. What more is requisite for the preservation of society? The great phenomenon of production analyzed and viewed in its proper light, explains all.

After the fear which you have testified, Sir, lest the produce of society should exceed in quantity what it can and will consume, it is natural that you should behold with terror its capitals increasing by parsimony; for the endeavour to employ capital causes an augmentation of productions,—new sources of accumulation— whence new productions arise: in short, you seem to fear that we should be suffocated beneath the overwhelming mass of our riches. This fear, I confess, does not torment me at all.

Was it for you, Sir, to renew the popular prejudices against those who do not expend their incomes in objects of luxury? You allow (page 351,) *that no permanent increase of wealth can take place without a previous increase of capital;* you allow (page 352), *that those who labour are consumers, as well as the unproductive consumers;* and yet you fear that if accumulation goes on, *it will be impossible to consume the still increasing quantity of commodities produced by these new labourers* (p. 353).

We must remove your vain terrors; but first permit me one reflection on the subject of modern political economy. It is of a nature to guide us on our way.

What is it that distinguishes us from the economists of the school of *Quesnay?* It is the scrupulous care with which we observe the concatenation of the facts which relate to wealth: it is the rigorous exactness which we impose on ourselves in describing them. Now, in order to see and to describe clearly, one must to the utmost of one's power remain a passive spectator. Not that we may not, ought not, indeed, sometimes to sigh at those operations, pregnant with ruinous effects, of which we are often the sad and impotent witnesses. The philanthropic historian is not prohibited from indulging in the mournful reflections which political iniquity frequently draws from him. But opinions and advice are not history; and, I insist, are not political economy. Our duty to the public is to inform it how and why one fact is the consequence of another. If it approves or fears the consequence, that is sufficient; it knows what it has to do: but *let us avoid exhortations.*

It appears, therefore, to me, that I ought not, after *Adam Smith,* to preach up parsimony; and that you should not, after Lord *Lauderdale,* extol dissipation. Let us confine ourselves to observing the manner in which things succeed, and are connected with each other in the accumulation of capitals.

In the first place, it is to be observed that the greater number of accumulations are necessarily slow. Every one, whatever be his income, has to live before he can save; and what I here call *living,* is, in general, so much the more expensive as the party is richer. In most cases and in professions, the support of a family and its establishment in life demands the whole income, and often the capital besides; and when there are some yearly savings, they are generally in a very small proportion to the capital actually employed. A man of business, with ten thousand pounds and a calling, gains, in ordinary cases, from twelve to fifteen hundred pounds per annum. Now with that capital, and a business of equal value, that is to say, with a fortune of twenty thousand pounds, he is economical if he only spends one thousand; he then saves annually only five hundred pounds or the twentieth part of his capital.

If this fortune be divided, as it often is, between two persons, one of whom supplies the capital, the other the industry, the saving will be still much less; because in this case two families are to live upon the united profits of the capital and industry, instead of one.* None but very great fortunes, of whatever nature, can allow great savings; and very great fortunes are rare in all countries. Therefore capital can never augment with a rapidity capable of producing sudden revolutions in industrious pursuits.

I am not sensible of the fears which caused you to say (p. 357), "That a country is always liable to an increase of the funds for the maintenance of labour faster than the increase of population." Neither am I afraid of the enormous surplus of productions to result from an augmentation of capital so slow in its nature. On the contrary, I see these new capitals, and the revenues which issue out of them, distribute themselves in the most advantageous way, amongst the producers. First, the capitalist, by augmenting his capital, increases his income, which invites him to multiply his enjoyments. A capital increased in the course of the year, purchases the following year a few more industrious services than before. These services being thus more in demand, are a little better paid; a greater number of the industrious find employment and reward for their faculties. They labour, and consume unproductively the produce of their labour; so that, if there is more produce created in consequence of this augmentation of capital, there are also more productions consumed. Now what is this but an increase of prosperity?

You say (p. 352, 360), "That if savings are made only with a view to increase capital—if capitalists do not add to their enjoyments by augmenting their incomes, they have no sufficient motive to save; for men do not save merely through philanthropy, and to make industry prosper." This is true, but what conclusion do you desire to draw from hence? If they save, I say, that they promote industry and production, and that this increase of production is distributed in the most advantageous manner to the public. If they do not save, I know not how to help it: but you cannot conclude from this that producers will be better off, for what the capitalists would have saved would nevertheless have been equally expended. In expending it unproductively, the expenditure has not been increased in amount. As to riches accumulated, without being reproductively consumed, such as the sums amassed in the miser's coffers, neither *Smith* nor I, nor any one, undertakes their defence; but they cause very little alarm; first, because they are always very inconsiderable, compared with the productive capital of a nation; and secondly, because their consumption is only suspended. All treasures get spent at last, productively or otherwise.

I cannot perceive on what account you look upon reproductive expenditure, such as that which is occasioned by digging canals, building shipping, erecting manufactories or barns, constructing machines, paying artists and artisans, as less favourable to producers than unproductive expenditure, or that which has for its object only the personal gratification of the prodigal. You say (p. 363), "While the farmers were disposed to consume the luxuries produced by the manufacturers, and the manufacturers those produced by the farmers, all would go on smoothly; but if either one or both the parties were disposed to save, with a view of bettering their condition and providing for their families in future, the state of things would be very different." That is to say, I presume, that all would go wrong! "The farmer, instead of indulging himself in ribbons, lace, and velvets, would be disposed to be satisfied with more simple clothing; but by this economy he would disable the manufacturer from purchasing the same amount of his produce: and for the returns of so much labour employed upon the land, and all greatly increased in productive power, there would evidently be no market. The manufacturer, in like manner, instead of indulging himself in sugar, grapes, and tobacco, might be disposed to save, with a view to the future, but would be totally unable to do so, owing to the parsimony of the farmers and the want of a demand for manufactures."

And a little farther on (p. 365), "The population required to provide simple clothing to such a society, with the assistance of good machinery, would be inconsiderable, and would absorb but a small portion of the proper surplus of rich and well-cultivated land. There would evidently therefore be a general want of demand both for produce and population: and while it is quite certain that an adequate passion for consumption (unproductive) may fully keep up the proper proportion between supply and demand, whatever may be the powers of production, it appears to be quite certain that a passion for accumulation must inevitably lead to a supply of commodities beyond what the structure and habits of such a society will permit to be consumed."

You go so far as to ask "what would become of the demand for commodities, if all consumption, except bread and water, were suspended for the next half year?"* and it is to me, by name, that you address this question.

In this passage and the foregoing, you assume implicitly as fact, that a production saved is abstracted from every species of consumption; although in all these discussions, in all the writings you attack, in those of *Adam Smith,* of Mr. *Ricardo,* in mine, and even in your own,† it is laid down that a production saved is so much substracted from unproductive consumption to be added to capital, that is to say, to the value that is consumed reproductively. "*What would become of commodities, if every species of consumption, except that of bread and water, were suspended for six months?*" Why, Sir, they would be sold for a value every bit as great; for, after all, what would be thereby added to the sum of capital, would buy meat, beer, coats, shirts, shoes, furniture, for that class of producers whose savings had so enabled them to make purchases. *But if they were to live on bread and water in order not to use their savings?* - - - That is to say, you suppose that they would generally bind themselves to an extravagant fast from mere wantonness, and without any object whatever!

What would you reply, Sir, to him who should place among the derangements that might happen in society, the case of the moon's falling on the earth? - - - - The thing is not physically impossible; it would only be requisite that the course of that planet in its orbit should be suspended, or even merely slackened by the approach of a comet. Nevertheless, I suspect you would be apt to discover something like impertinence in such a proposition; and I must own I think you would be very excusable.

Philosophy, indeed, does not reject the method of carrying principles to their extreme consequences, in order to exaggerate and discover their errors; but this exaggeration itself is an error when the nature of things itself presents continually increasing obstacles to the supposed excess, and thus renders the supposition inadmissible. To the disciples of *Adam Smith,* who think that saving is beneficial, you oppose the inconveniences of an excessive saving; but here the excess carries its remedy along with it. Wherever capital becomes too abundant, the interest which capitalists derive from it becomes too small to balance the privations which they impose upon themselves by their economy. It becomes more and more difficult to find good securities for investing money, which is then placed in foreign securities. The simple course of nature stops many accumulations. A great part of those which occur in families in good circumstances are stopped the moment it becomes necessary to provide for the establishment of children. The incomes of the fathers being reduced by this circumstance, they lose the means of accumulating at the same time that they lose part of the motives which induced them to save. Many accumulations are also stopped at the decease of the proprietor. An estate is divided amongst the heirs and legatees, whose situation is different from that of the deceased, and who often dissipate part of the inheritance instead of increasing it. That portion which the fiscal department seizes, is very sure to be dissipated, for the state does not employ it reproductively.

The prodigality and inexperience of many individuals, who lose part of their capitals in ill-concerted schemes, require to be balanced by the economy of many others. Every thing tends to convince us, that in what respects accumulation, as well as other matters, there is much less danger in leaving things to take their natural course, than in endeavouring to give them a forced direction.

You say (p. 495), "That in some cases it is contrary to sound principles of political economy to advise saving." I repeat, Sir, that *sound* political economy is *not apt to advise;* it shews what a capital judiciously employed adds to the power of industry, in the same manner as sound agricultural knowledge teaches what a well-managed irrigation adds to the power of the soil; and after this it leaves to the world the truths which it demonstrates; of which every one is to avail himself according to his intelligence and capacity.

All that is required, Sir, of a man so enlightened as yourself, is, not to propagate the popular error, that prodigality is more favourable to producers than economy.* Mankind is already but too much disposed to sacrifice the future to the present. The principle of all amelioration is, on the contrary, the sacrifice of momentary temptations to future welfare. This is the first foundation of all virtue as well as of all wealth. The man who loses his character by violating a trust; he who ruins his health by giving way to his desires; and he who spends to-day his means of gain for to-morrow, are all equally deficient in economy: hence it has been said, with much reason, that vice is nothing, at the end of the account, but a bad calculation.

Notes

[*] Does not the farmer, who sells a sack of corn for thirty shillings, and buys a piece of calico at thirty shillings, exchange his corn for the stuff? and does not the manufacturer, who buys a sack of corn at thirty shillings, being the price of his piece of stuff, exchange that piece for a sack of corn?

[*] That I may not incur the charge of misrepresentation, while I am merely endeavouring to compress and render more perspicuous the meaning of the worthy professor, I copy the exact passages. "If commodities were only to be compared and exchanged with each other, then, indeed, it would be true that, if they were all increased in their proper proportions to any extent, they would continue to bear among themselves the same relative value; but if we compare them, as we certainly ought to do, with the numbers and wants of the consumers, then a great increase of produce with comparatively stationary numbers, and with wants diminished by parsimony, must necessarily occasion a great fall of value estimated in labour, so that the same produce, though it might have *cost* the same quantity of labour, would no longer *command* the same quantity"....p. 355. "It is asserted that effectual demand is nothing more than the offering one commodity in exchange for another. But is this all that is necessary to effectual demand? Though each commodity may have cost the same quantity of labour and capital in its production, and they may be exactly equivalent to each other in exchange, yet why may not both be so plentiful as not to command more labour, or but very little more than they have cost; and in this case, would the demand for them be effectual? Would it be such as to encourage their continued production? Unquestionably not." p. 355, 356.

[*] That is, according to the English expression: *when they* (productions) *do not command the same quantity of labour as before.*

[†] This demonstration, by the bye, completely overthrows an assertion of Mr. Malthus, *that cheapness is always (must be) at the expense of profits* (p. 370), and consequently all the reasoning which he has built on this foundation. It is also fatal to all that part of Mr. Ricardo's doctrine, in which he flatters himself that he has proved, that the *costs of production,* and not the proportion of *supply* and *demand,* regulates the prices of goods. He identifies the *costs of production* with the *production* itself, whereas they are completely opposed to each other, and the former are diminished in proportion to the increase of the latter.

[*] Some people imagine that when capital is employed in an undertaking the portion of this capital which is employed in purchasing raw materials, is not employed in purchasing productive services. This is an error. Raw material itself is a product, which has no other value than that which has been imparted to it by productive services, which have made it a product; have given it a value. When raw material is of no value, it employs no part of capital: when it must be paid for, this payment is only to reimburse the productive services which have created its value.

[*] The profits which are made by a person who carries on any undertaking, are the reward of the labour and talents which he exerts in his business. He only continues this business while it produces such an income that he cannot expect a better in any other employment. He is one of the necessary producers, and his profits form part of the necessary charges of production.

[*] This happens in France much more frequently than in England, where the rate of the profits of industry and interest of capital is too low in ordinary employments for the former to suffice for the support of a family who have no capital.

[*] "What an accumulation of commodities! what a prodigious market, according to M. Say (says Mr. Malthus), would this event

occasion!" The learned professor here totally mistakes the meaning of the word *accumulation:* accumulation is not *non-consumption;* it is the substitution of reproductive consumption for that which is unproductive. Besides, I never said that a product *saved* was a market opened; I said that a product *made* was a market opened for another product; and that is true, whether the value of it be unproductively consumed, or whether it be added to the savings of its proprietor, that is to say, to the reproductive expenditure which he intends to make.

[†] "It must be allowed that the produce annually saved is as regularly consumed as that which is annually spent, but that it is consumed by a different set of people." —*Malthus's Principles of Political Economy,* p. 31.

[*] "When there is more capital than is necessary in a country, to recommend saving is contrary to all principles of political economy. It is like recommending marriage to a people perishing with famine." —*Principles of Political Economy,* p. 495. How came Mr. Malthus not to perceive that marriage gives birth to children, and consequently to new wants; whilst capitals have no wants, but, on the contrary, possess the means of satisfying them?

LETTER III.

Sir,

We have hitherto founded our discussions upon the supposition of an indefinite liberty, allowing a nation to carry to the utmost extent production of every description; and it appears to me that I have proved that if this hypothesis could be realized, a nation so circumstanced would be able to purchase all that it could produce. From this faculty, and from the natural and perpetual desire of men to ameliorate their condition, an infinite multiplication of individuals and of gratifications would infallibly arise.

But the course of events is different. Nature and the abuses of social order have set limits to this faculty of production; and the examination of those limits, by leading us back into the existing world, will serve to prove the truth of the doctrine established in my treatise on political economy, that the obstacles to production are the real and sole impediments to the sale and disposal of produce.

I do not pretend to point out the whole of the obstacles by which production is impeded. Many of these impediments will manifest themselves during the progress of the science of political economy; others, perhaps, will never be ascertained, but many of great influence may already be observed, both in the natural or political order of things.

In the natural order, the production of alimentary commodities is more rigidly limited than that of furniture and clothing. Although mankind stand in need of a much greater quantity, in weight and value, of alimentary goods, than of all other sorts of produce together, yet commodities of this description cannot be brought from any considerable distance, for they are difficult to transport, and the care of them is expensive. As to those which may grow upon the territory of a nation, they are confined within boundaries, which the improvement of agriculture, and increase of capitals engaged therein may certainly extend,* but which will always be sure to exist. *Arthur*

Young thinks that France does not produce more than half the alimentary produce which she is capable of producing. Suppose he is right in this; suppose even that with a more perfect agricultural system, France were to obtain double her present quantity of rural produce, without employing more agricultural labourers,† she would then possess 45 millions of inhabitants at liberty to devote themselves to other occupations. Her manufactures would find better markets in the country than at present, because the country would be more productive, and the surplus would be sold among the manufacturing population itself. People would not be worse fed than at present, but they would in general be better provided with articles of manufacture; with better dwellings, more furniture, finer clothing, and with objects of utility, instruction, and entertainment, which are now reserved for a very small number of people. The rest of the population is still rude and barbarous.

But in proportion as the manufacturing class increased, alimentary produce would become more in demand and dearer with relation to manufactures. The latter would produce diminished profits and wages, which would discourage those engaged in such branches of industry; hence it is easy to conceive how the restrictions which nature imposes on agricultural production, limit the produce of manufacture. But this effect, like all which happens naturally and results from the nature of things, would be very gradual, and attended with fewer inconveniences than any other possible combination.

Admitting the limits thus set by nature to the production of provisions, and, indirectly, of all other commodities, it may be asked how it happens that very industrious countries, such as England, where capital abounds and communications are easy, find the sale of their goods impeded long before their agricultural produce has attained its utmost limit. Is there then some unsoundness—some concealed disease, which preys upon them? - - - - There are probably several, which will successively show themselves; but I already perceive one—immense—fatal—and deserving the most serious attention.

Suppose some individual, a collector of public revenue for instance, were to take up his residence in the neighbourhood of each commercial, manufacturing, or agricultural establishment; and that this man without increasing the goodness of the produce, its utility, or the quality by which it becomes an object of desire and demand, were nevertheless to increase the costs of its production: what, I ask, would be the consequence? The value which is set on a commodity, even where the means of obtaining it exist,* depends on the enjoyment and utility which it is expected to afford. In proportion as its price rises, many persons cease to think it worth the expense which it occasions, and thus the number of its purchasers is diminished.

Besides, taxes do not augment the profits of the producer, although they increase the price of every production: the incomes of the producers become insufficient to purchase the produce, the moment its price is raised by the circumstance which I have just described.

Let us represent this effect by numbers, in order to pursue it to its remotest consequences. It will be well worth the trouble of examination, if it enable us to discern one of the principal causes of the evil which menances every industrious nation of the earth. Already the distresses of England forewarn other countries of the miseries which are reserved for them. They will be more painful wherever a more robust temperament excites to a greater developement of industry; the happiest effects will result from this, if it be left at full liberty; if it be restrained, then terrible convulsions will be the consequence.

If the manufacturer who produces a piece of stuff, after dividing between his assistants and himself a sum of thirty shillings for the productive services which have been employed in the production of the piece, is moreover compelled to pay six shillings to the receiver of taxes, either he must cease to make stuffs, or he must sell them for 36 shillings the piece.* But when this piece of stuff comes thus to be valued at 36 shillings, those who produced it, and have only received altogether 30 shillings, will only be able to buy five-sixths of the same article of which they could have previously purchased the whole; he who before could purchase a yard, must now be restricted to five-sixths of a yard, and so on.

The producer of corn who pays to another receiver a tax of six shillings on a sack of corn, of which the productive services have cost 30, must now obtain 36 for his sack instead of 30. It follows that the producers of corn and stuffs, when in want of either of those articles, can only acquire by their gains five-sixths of their productions.

As this effect is seen in these two commodities reciprocally, it may also take place in other articles. Without changing the state of the question, it is easy to suppose that producers, in whatever species of production they may be occupied, have occasion for liquors, colonial produce, lodgings, amusements, and objects of convenience and of luxury. These commodities they will find dearer than they can afford, with incomes such as they now enjoy, according to the rank which they occupy among the producers. Upon the hypothesis which we have taken for our example, there will always remain a sixth part of the produce unsold.

True it is, that the six shillings taken by the collector go to some one, and that those whom the collector represents (public functionaries, military men, or public creditors) may employ this money in obtaining the remaining sixth part, either of the sack of corn, or the piece of stuff, or of any other production. This indeed is what actually happens. But let it be observed that this consumption is entirely at the expense of the producers; and that if the collector, or those by whom he is authorized, consume a sixth part of the produce, the producers are thereby compelled to live upon the remaining five-sixths.

This you will allow; but, at the same time, I shall be told that any one may live upon five-sixths of what he produces. I am willing to admit that; but permit me to ask whether you think the producer could live equally well if two-sixths, instead of one, or one-third of his produce, were demanded from him? — No; but still he would live. - - - Ah! you think he would live! Then would he still *live* in case two-thirds were wrested from him?—then three-fourths?—But I perceive you do not attempt to reply.

Now, Sir, I flatter myself that my answers to the most urgent objections offered by you and M. Sismondi will be easily comprehended. "If, by creating new productions, (say you,) we are enabled to consume them, or to exchange them for others of which there exists a superabundance, and thus to procure markets for both, why then are not such new productions created? Is capital wanting? Capital abounds: every where undertakings are sought for in which it may be advantageously employed: it is evident (you affirm) that there are no longer any such," (p. 499); "that all kinds of commerce are already overstocked with capital and labourers, who all offer their produce under prime cost," M. Sismondi assures us.*

I am not quite prepared to say, that to follow the useful arts is a fool's trade; but you will allow, gentlemen, that if ever it should become so, the consequence would not be different from that which you are lamenting. To buy the superabundant produce, it would be requisite to create other produce: but if the producers were placed in too disadvantageous a situation; if, after exerting the productive means sufficient for producing an ox, they were to produce only a sheep, and for this sheep, in exchange for any other kind of produce, were only to gain the same quantity of utility which exists in a sheep, who would go on producing under such disadvantages? The persons engaged in such an undertaking would have made a bad business of it: they would have expended a value which the utility of their produce would not suffice to reimburse; whoever should be silly enough to create another production sufficient to purchase the former, would have to contend with the same disadvantages, and would involve himself in the same difficulties. The benefit which he might derive from his production would not indemnify him for its expenses; and whatever he might buy with this production would be of no greater value. Then, indeed, the workman would no longer be able to live by his labour, and would become burthensome to his parish;* then the manufacturer, unable to live on his profits, would renounce his business. He would buy annuities, or go abroad in search of a better situation, a more lucrative employment, *or, what is* *exactly equivalent,* a production at less expense.† If he were there to meet with other inconveniences, he would again seek another theatre for his talents; and different nations would be seen pouring forth upon each other their capitals and their labourers; that is to say, all that is requisite to raise human society to the highest pitch of prosperity, if it understood its true interests, and the means by which they may be promoted.

I shall not attempt to point out the parts of this picture which apply more particularly to your country, Sir, or to any other; but I leave it for your consideration, and that of all well-meaning men who exert themselves to promote the welfare of the interesting, laborious, and useful part of mankind. Why do the savages of the new world, whose precarious subsistence depends on the flight of an arrow, neglect to build villages, and to inclose and cultivate lands? Because this kind of life demands labour too assiduous and painful. They are in the wrong; they calculate ill, for the privations they endure are far less tolerable than the constraints which a well-regulated social life would impose upon them. But if this social life were a galley, in which, after rowing with all their strength for sixteen hours out of the twenty-four, they were able to obtain only a piece of bread insufficient to feed them, they might indeed be excused for disliking social life. Now whatever renders the condition of the producer, the essential party in every society, more painful, tends to destroy the vital principle of the social body; to reduce a civilized people to a savage state; to introduce a state of things in which less is produced and less consumed; to destroy civilization, which is extended in proportion to the increase of the quantity of production and consumption. You observe, in several places, "that man is naturally indolent, and that it betrays great ignorance of his nature *to suppose that he will always consume all he can produce*" (p. 503). You are right, indeed; but I maintain no other doctrine when I say that the utility of productions is no longer worth the productive services, at the rate at which we are compelled to pay for them.

You appear convinced of this truth where you say, on another occasion (p. 342), "A tax will entirely put an end to the production of a commodity, if no one of the society is disposed to value it at a price equal to the new conditions of its supply." And this inherent vice (of costing in charges of production more than it is worth) the commodity carries with it to the ends of the earth. It is every where too dear to command what it has cost, because it must be purchased by productive services equivalent to those employed in its production.

Another consideration, by no means unimportant is, that the costs of production are augmented not only by multiplied duties, by the dearness of articles of every sort, but by the habits which are produced by a vicious political system. If the progress of luxury and enormous emoluments—if the facility of obtaining illegitimate profits through favour and influence in contracts and financial operations, force the manufacturer, the merchant, the real producer, to require profits disproportioned to the services which they render to the production, in order to maintain their rank in society, then all these abuses tend to raise, from other causes, the costs of production, and consequently the price of productions, above the value of their actual utility. The consumption of commodities consequently becomes more limited; in order to acquire them, a greater quantity of productive services must be employed in the creation of another production: the charges of production must be increased. Consider then, Sir, how extensive are the evils produced by encouraging useless expenses, and multiplying unproductive consumers.

The rapid sale of articles offered at a cheap rate by means of expeditious methods of production, proves how truly the cost of production is the real impediment to the sale of goods. If the price be reduced one fourth, it is found that a double quantity is sold. The reason is, that every one is then enabled to acquire it with less labour, less costs of production. When under the Continental system it was necessary to pay five francs for a pound of sugar, whether the money were applied to the production of the sugar, or of any other commodity to be exchanged for it, France was able to purchase only fourteen millions of pounds.* Now that sugar is cheap, we consume eighty millions of pounds per annum, being about three pounds for each person. At Cuba, where sugar is still cheaper, they consume above thirty pounds for every free person.†

Let us then agree upon a truth which on every side presses on our notice. To levy excessive duties, with or without the participation of a national representation, or by means of a mock representation, no matter which, is to augment the costs of production without increasing the utility of the produce, without adding any thing to the satisfaction which the consumer may derive from it, and to impose a fine on production—on that which enables society to exist. And as among producers some are more advantageously situated than others for throwing upon their competitors all the burthen of circumstances, they fall heavier on some classes than on others. A capitalist can often withdraw his capital from one employment to place it in another, or to send it abroad. The proprietor of a concern may often be rich enough to be able to suspend his operations for a time. Besides, as long as the capitalist and the master can make their own terms with the workman, the latter is obliged to work constantly, and at any price, even when the employment does not procure him a subsistence. Thus do the excessive charges of production reduce several classes of certain nations to the necessity of confining their consumption to articles the most indispensable to their existence, and the lowest classes of all to die of want. Now, Sir, is not this, upon your own principle,* the most shocking and barbarous of all the methods of reducing the numbers of mankind?†

We now come to the objection in which there is, perhaps, the greatest force, because it is supported by an imposing example. In the United States, the obstacles to production are few, the taxes are light; and there, as in all other places, merchandize abounds, for which there exists no demand. "These difficulties," you say,‡ "cannot be attributed to the cultivation of poor land, restrictions upon commerce, and excess of taxation. Something else, therefore, is necessary to the continued increase of wealth, besides an increase in the power of producing."

Well! will you believe it, Sir? it is the very *power of production* itself, at least for the present, of which the Americans are in want, to enable them to dispose of the overflowing productions of their commerce to advantage.

The favourable situation of this people, during a long war, in which they have almost always enjoyed the advantage of neutrality, has turned their industry, and capitals, far too exclusively to external and maritime commerce. The Americans are enterprising; their voyages are cheaply performed; they have introduced into navigation long courses, and various accelerating manœuvres, which by shortening voyages, reduce their expense, and correspond with those improvements in the arts which diminish the costs of production; in short, the Americans have drawn to themselves all the maritime commerce which the English have not been able to engross; they have, for many years, been the intermediate agents between all the Continental powers of Europe and the rest of the world. Their success has even exceeded that of the English wherever those nations have been competitors, as in China.

What has been the result? An excessive abundance of those commodities which are obtained by commercial and maritime industry; and when the general peace at length opened the highway of the ocean to all nations, the French and Dutch ships rushed with a kind of madness into the midst of a career thus newly opened to them; and in their ignorance of the actual state of countries beyond sea—of their agriculture, arts, population, and resources for buying and consuming—these ships, escaped from a tedious detention, carried in abundance the produce of the Continent of Europe to all ports, presuming that the other nations of the globe would be eager to possess those commodities after their long separation from Europe.

But in order to purchase this extraordinary supply, it would have been requisite for these countries to create immediately extraordinary quantities of produce of their own; for, once more I repeat it, the difficulty at New York, at Baltimore, the Havannah, Rio-Janeiro, or Buenos-Ayres, is not to consume European manufactures. They would consume them very willingly if they could pay for them. But the Europeans required payment in cottons, tobaccos, sugars, and rice; but this demand even enhanced their prices: and as, notwithstanding the dearness of these commodities, and of money, which is also merchandize, it was necessary to take them or return without payment, these very articles, thus rendered scarce in their original country, became more abundant in Europe, and at length so completely overstocked the European markets, that a sufficient price could not be obtained for them, although the consumption of Europe had greatly increased since the peace: hence the disadvantageous returns which we have witnessed. But suppose for an instant that the agricultural and manufactured produce of both North and South America had suddenly become very considerable at the time of the peace, in that case the people of those countries, being more numerous, and producing more, would easily have purchased all the European cargoes, and furnished a variety of returns at a cheap rate.

This effect will, I doubt not, take place with respect to the United States, when they are enabled to add to the objects of exchange furnished by their maritime commerce, a greater quantity of their agricultural produce,* and perhaps some articles of manufacture also. Their cultivation is extending; their manufactures multiply; and as a natural consequence their population increases with astonishing rapidity. In a few years the whole of their varied industry will form a mass of produce, amongst which will be found more articles calculated to furnish profitable returns, or at least profits of which the Americans will employ a part in the purchase of European merchandize.

Merchandize produced by Europeans at a less expense than it can be made for in America will be carried to the United States; and goods which the soil and industry of America produce cheaper than they can be had elsewhere, will be carried home in exchange. The nature of demands will determine the nature of productions; each nation will prefer engaging in that kind of production in which it has the greatest success, that is, which it produces at the smallest expense; and the result will be exchanges mutually and permanently advantageous. But these commercial ameliorations can only be brought about by time. The talents and experience which the arts require are not acquired in a few months; years are necessary. The Americans will not discover in what manufactures they can succeed until after several attempts.* Then those particular manufactures will no longer be carried to them; but the profits which they will derive from this production will enable them to purchase other European produce.

On the other hand, agricultural speculations, however rapid may be their extension, can only by very slow degrees, present by their produce markets to the productions of Europe. As fast as culture and civilization extend beyond the Allegany mountains, into Kentucky and the territories of Indiana and the Illinois, the first gains are employed in the subsistence of the colonists as they arrive from the states more anciently peopled, and in building their habitations. The profits which exceed these first wants, enable them to clear a greater quantity of land; the next gains are employed in manufacturing their own produce for local consumption: and only the savings of a fourth order can be applied to the manufacture and fabrication of the produce of the soil for distant consumption. It is not until this latter state of things takes place that new states begin to offer markets for Europeans; this cannot be in their earliest infancy: their population must have had time to increase, and their agricultural produce must have become sufficiently abundant to oblige them to exchange it at a distance for other value. Afterwards, and by the natural progress of things, instead of exporting raw produce, they export produce which has received some preparation, and which consequently, comprising a greater value in a less bulk, is adapted to bear the expense of carriage. Such produce will one day come to Europe from New Orleans, a city destined to become one of the greatest marts in the world.

This point has not yet been attained; is it then wonderful that the productions of the United States have not yet afforded markets sufficient for the commercial efforts which followed the peace? Is it extraordinary that the commercial produce brought by the Americans themselves into their ports, at the conclusion of an excessive developement of their nautical industry, should yet remain there in superabundance?

You see, Sir, that there is nothing in this fact but what is quite conformable to the doctrine of your antagonists.

Returning to the painful situation in which all kinds of industry is at present placed in Europe, I might add to the discouragement resulting from the excessive increase of the charges of production, the disorders which such charges occasion in the production, distribution, and consumption of the values produced; disorders which frequently bring into the market a supply superior to the demand, and at the same time drive out of it much which might have been sold, and the prices of which would have been employed in the purchase of the former. Certain producers endeavour to recover by the quantity of what they produce a part of the value consumed by the revenue. Some productive services are able to escape from the avidity of the fiscal agents, as often happens with the productive services of capital, which frequently contrives to obtain the same interest, while lands, buildings, and industry are oppressed. Sometimes a workman who finds it difficult to maintain his family, endeavours by excessive toil to make up for the low price of his labour. Are not these causes which derange the natural order of production, and which occasion productions of some kinds to exceed what would have taken place, if the wants of the consumers alone had been considered? All objects of consumption are not necessary to us in the same degree. Before we reduce our consumption of corn to one half, we reduce our consumption of meat to a fourth, and our consumption of sugar to nothing. There are capitals so engaged in certain undertakings, particularly in manufactures, that the proprietors often consent to lose the interest, and sacrifice the profits of their industry, and continue to labour merely to support the establishment until more favourable times, and to preserve their utensils and connexions: sometimes they are apprehensive of losing good workmen, whom the suspension of employment would compel to disperse; the humanity of the proprietors is sufficient, in some instances, to carry on a manufacture which is no longer in demand. Hence arise disorders in the progress of production and consumption, still more grievous than those which originate in the prohibitions of the revenue or the vicissitudes of the seasons. Hence we see inconsiderate productions—hence recourse is had to rainous means—hence commercial establishments are overthrown.

At the same time I must remark, that although the evil is great, it probably seems greater than it is. The commodities which overstock all the markets in the world, may strike the eye by their magnitude in a mass, terrify the commercial world by their depreciation in value, and yet constitute only a very small part of the merchandizes of every sort made and consumed. There is no warehouse but would speedily be emptied, if every species of production of which its contents are made up, were to cease simultaneously in every part of the world. Besides, it has been observed, that the slightest excess of supply beyond the demand is sufficient to produce a considerable alteration in price. It is remarked in the *Spectator* (No. 200), that when the harvest exceeds by a tenth what is ordinarily consumed, the corn falls to half its price. *Dalrymple** makes an analogous observation. We must not then be surprised if a slight excess should be frequently represented as an excessive superabundance.

This superabundance, as I have already remarked, is also occasioned in part by the ignorance of producers or traders on the nature and extent of the demand in the places to which goods are consigned. Of late years there have been many speculations hazarded, because there have been many new relations between different nations. *Data* were every where wanting to serve as the foundation of good calculations; but does it follow that because many affairs have been unprofitable, that others with better information may not succeed? I venture to predict that as new relations shall grow old, and reciprocal wants be more justly appreciated, the markets will cease to be glutted, and permanent connexions of mutual profit will be established.

But at the same time it is expedient to diminish gradually, and as far as the circumstances of every state will allow, the general and permanent inconveniencies which spring from too expensive a productive system. We ought to be firmly convinced that the more others gain, the more easily we shall sell our produce; that there is only one way to gain, namely, to produce, either by our own labour, or by that of the capital or lands we possess; that unproductive consumers are only substitutes for productive consumers; that the more producers, the more consumers there are; that, by the same rule, every nation is interested in the prosperity of every other nation, and that all are interested in having the easiest communications with each other, for every difficulty is equivalent to an increase of expense.

Such is the doctrine established in my writings, and which, I acknowledge, does not appear to me to have been shaken. I took up my pen to defend it, not because it is mine (the self-love of an author would be contemptible where such great interests are concerned), but because it is eminently social, and points out to mankind the sources of true wealth and the danger of drying them up. The rest of this doctrine is no less useful, because it teaches that capital and land are only productive when they are become respected property; that the poor man is interested in defending the property of the rich; that he is consequently interested in the preservation of good order, because a subversion, which could only yield him a temporary plunder, would deprive him of a permanent income. When we study political economy as it ought to be studied; when we have once perceived that the most useful truths rest on the most certain principles; we have nothing so much at heart as to place these principles within the reach of every understanding. Let us not augment their difficulties by useless abstraction; let us not recommence the folly of the economists of the 18th century by endless discussions on the *net produce* of lands; let us describe the manner in which facts occur, and expose the chain which connects them; it is then that our writings will acquire a great *practical* utility, and the public will be truly indebted to writers who are, like you, Sir, possessed of such ample means of enlightening them.

Notes

[*] The principal obstacles to agricultural improvement in France are, first, the residence of the rich proprietors and great capitalists in towns, and particularly in an immense capital; they cannot acquire a knowledge of the ameliorations in which their capitals might be employed; nor can they watch over the application of those funds so as to obtain a corresponding increase of income. Secondly, it would be in vain for any particular secluded canton to double its produce; it

can now scarcely get rid of what it already produces, for want of good cross roads, and industrious neighbouring towns. Industrious towns consume rural produce, and fabricate in exchange articles of manufacture, which containing greater value in a less compass can be carried to a greater distance. This is the principal impediment to the increase of French agriculture. The multiplication of small navigable canals, and cross-roads well maintained, would greatly augment the value of rural produce. But these objects would require local administrations chosen by the inhabitants, and intent only on the good of the country. The possibility of markets exists, but nothing is done to secure the benefit of them. Magistrates chosen in the interest of the central authority, become almost invariably fiscal or political agents, or what is still worse, agents of police.

[†] This supposition is very admissible, since in England three fourths of the population inhabit towns, and consequently are not employed in agricultural pursuits. A country supporting 60 millions of inhabitants, might therefore be well cultivated by 15 millions of agricultural labourers; at which number the cultivators of France are now actually estimated.

[*] The means of acquisition are the profits which each individual derives from his industry, his capital, and his lands. Consumers who have neither industry, capital, nor land, spend only what they are able to obtain from the profits of those who have. In every case, the income of each individual has a limit; and thoughthe possessors of very large incomes can sacrifice a great quantity of money for very trivial enjoyments, it must be allowed that the dearer any gratification is, the less it is considered indispensable.

[*] If he reduce the quality, it will be equivalent to an increase in the price.

[*] Nouveaux Principes, liv. iv. chap. 4.

[*] The workman can only labour constantly whilst his work pays for his subsistence; and when his subsistence becomes too dear, it no longer suits the master to employ him. It may then be said, in the

language of political economy, that the workman no longer *offers* (or supplies) his productive services, although in fact he is most anxious for employment; but his offer is not acceptable on the only lasting conditions on which it can be made.

[†] Mr. Ricardo insists that, notwithstanding taxes and other charges, there is always as much industry as capital employed; and that all capital saved is always employed, because the interest is not suffered to be lost. On the contrary, many savings are not invested, when it is difficult to find employment for them, and many which are employed are dissipated in ill-calculated undertakings. Besides, Mr. Ricardo is completely refuted, not only by what happened to us in 1813, when the errors of Government ruined all commerce, and when the interest of money fell very low, for want of good opportunities of employing it; but by our present circumstances, when capitals are quietly sleeping in the coffers of their proprietors. The bank of France alone possesses 223 millions of specie (about nine millions of pounds sterling) in its chests, which is more than double the amount of its notes in circulation, and six times what prudence would consider necessary to reserve for the ordinary course of its payments.

[*] See the Report on the Situation of France, made in 1813, by the then Minister of the Interior. He was interested in concealing this diminution of commerce.

[†] Humbolt, Essai sur la Nouvelle Espague, tom. iii. p. 183.

[*] Malthus on Population, book ii. ch. 13, 5th ed.

[†] Mr. Malthus, convinced that certain classes are serviceable to society on account of what they consume alone, without producing any thing, would look upon the payment of the whole, or a great part of the English national debt, as a misfortune. On the contrary, this operation would, in my opinion, be very desirable for England; for the consequence would be, that the public creditors, being paid off, would find means to derive an income from their capitals; that the payers of taxes would themselves spend the 40 millions sterling

which they now pay to the public creditors; that the taxes being diminished by 40 millions sterling, all productions would be cheaper; that consumption would consequently be greatly extended, and would afford employment to the workmen instead of the sabre blows which are now dealt out to them; and I own I see nothing in these results to alarm the friends of the public weal.

[‡] P. 498.

[*] The commercial productions with which they furnish France, are sugar from India, China, and the Havannah, coffee, tea, nankeens, indigo, ginger, rhubarb, cinnamon, raw silk, and pepper.—Those of their soil and their arts are, cotton, tobacco, potash, rice, bark, whale oil, and dye woods.

[*] The manufactures which a new nation may execute to the greatest advantage, are, in general, those which consist in preparing raw materials of their own growth, or imported at a small expense. It is not probable that the United States will ever supply Europe with cloth; but they will perhaps furnish her with manufactured tobaccos, and refined sugars; perhaps they may even establish cotton-manufactories on better terms than England.

[*] Considerations on the Policy of Entails, p. 14.

LETTER IV.

Sir,

I expected to have found in your *"Principles of Political Economy,"* something calculated to settle public opinion on the subject of machinery, and all those inventions for facilitating production by which manual labour is saved, and the quantity of produce is increased without any addition to the costs of production. I was in hopes to meet with such definite principles, such exact reasoning, as would command conviction; to which your *Essay on Population* has accustomed the public; - - - - but the present is not the Essay on Population.

It seems to me, (for I am sometimes reduced to the necessity of using this form of expression after having read your demonstrations)—it appears to me that you recognize only one advantage in the use of expeditious methods of production; namely, that of multiplying produce to such a degree, that even when its selling price is diminished, the total value of the quantity produced still exceeds the value of the quantity produced before the introduction of the improvements.* The advantage which you particularize is incontestable; and it had previously been observed, that the total value of the cotton manufactures, as well as the number of workmen employed in that pursuit, was singularly increased since the introduction of the improved methods of manufacture. An analogous observation had been made with respect to the printing-press, the machine employed in the multiplication of books, a branch of produce which now employs (besides authors) a much greater number of industrious persons than formerly, when books were copied by hand, and produces a sum far greater than when books were more expensive.

But this very substantial advantage is only one amongst many which nations have derived from the use of machines. It only refers to certain articles of produce, the consumption of which was capable of sufficient extension to counterbalance the diminution of price; but there is in the introduction of machinery an advantage common to every economical and expeditive process; an advantage which would be felt, even where the consumption of the article produced was not susceptible of any increase; an advantage which ought to be fully appreciated in the *principles* of political economy. You will excuse my returning to some elementary notions for the purpose of clearly explaining myself on this point.

Machines and *tools* are both productions which, as soon as they are produced, become *capital*, and are employed in the production of other articles. The only difference which exists between machines and tools is, that the former are complex tools, and the latter are simple machines. As there are neither tools nor machines which *create* power, they must be considered as means by which we transmit an action, a vivid force, which we have the power of directing to an object intended to be modified by that force. Thus a hand-hammer is a tool by means whereof we employ the muscular force of a man, in certain cases to beat out a leaf of gold; and the hammers of a great forge are likewise tools by means whereof we employ a fall of water in flattening iron bars.

The employment of a power gratuitously furnished by nature, does not take away from a machine its quality as a tool. Weight multiplied by quickness, which constitutes the power of a goldbeater's hammer, is no less a physical power of nature, than the weight of the water which falls from a mountain.

What is the whole of our industry, but the employment of the laws of nature? *It is by obeying nature,* says Bacon, *that we learn to command her.* What difference do you perceive between knitting-needles and a stocking-frame, but that the latter is a tool more complex and more efficient than the needles, but, in fact, applying, to greater or less advantage, the properties of metal, and the power of the lever, to fabricate the vestments with which we cover our feet and legs?

The question is, therefore, reduced to this:—Is it advantageous for man to take into his hands a tool more powerful, capable of doing a much greater quantity of work, or of doing it much better, in preference to another tool of a gross and imperfect construction, with which he must work more slowly, with greater toil, and less perfection?

I should be doing injustice to your good sense and that of our readers, were I to doubt of the universal answer.

The perfection of our tools is connected with the perfection of our species. It is this which constitutes the difference which we observe between ourselves and the savages of the South Seas, who have hatchets of flint, and sewing-needles made of fish-bones. It is no longer permitted to a writer on political economy to recommend the prohibition of such means as chance or genius may furnish us with; even for the express purpose of reserving more labour for our workmen: he would soon find all his own reasoning employed to prove that we ought, retrograding instead of advancing in the career of civilization, to relinquish, successively, all the discoveries we have made, and render our arts more imperfect for the purpose of multiplying our toils, and of lessening our enjoyments.

Undoubtedly there are inconveniences inseparable from the transition from one order of things to another, even from an imperfect order to one which is better. What wise man would wish to abolish, all at once, the prohibitions which oppress industry, and the customs and duties which impede the intercourse of nations, prejudicial as they are to general prosperity? On these subjects, the duty of well-informed persons consists, not in suggesting motives for preventing and proscribing every species of change, under pretext of the inconveniences which it may produce; but in appreciating those inconveniences; in pointing out the practicable means of averting or mitigating them, in order to facilitate the adoption of a desirable amelioration.

The inconvenience, in this case, is a shifting of income, which, when sudden, is always more or less distressing to that class whose revenues are diminished. The introduction of machines diminishes (sometimes, but not always) the income of the classes who derive their subsistence from their corporeal and manual faculties, and augments the revenues of those whose resources consist in their intellectual faculties and their capitals. In other terms, machines which abridge labour, being, in general, more complex, demand more considerable capitals. The person who uses them is, therefore, obliged to purchase more of what we call *the productive services of capital,* and requires less of what we call the *productive services of labourers.* At the same time, as they require in their general and particular management perhaps more extensive combinations and more sedulous attention, they require more of that species of service whence the profit of the proprietor is derived. Cotton-spinning, by means of the small wheel as it was formerly carried on by many families in Normandy, scarcely merits the name of a factory; whilst a cotton-mill on a large scale is a factory of the first consequence.

But the most important, though not the most generally perceived, effect resulting from the use of machinery, and, in general, from every expediting process, is the increase of income which is thereby acquired by the consumers of the articles produced; an increase which costs nothing to anybody, and merits some more detailed examination.

	fr.
If people were now to grind their corn as it was ground by the ancients, by manual labour, I estimate that it would require twenty men to grind as much meal as is ground by a pair of stones in our mills. These twenty men, constantly employed, would cost, in the neighbourhood of Paris, 40 francs per day; and counting 300 working-days in the year would cost annually	12,000
The machine and the grinding-stones would cost originally 20,000 francs, of which the annual interest is	1,000
It is not probable that any person would undertake such a business, unless it would bring in annually about	3,000
The making of the meal by hand, which may now be ground in a year by a pair of millstones, would cost by this method about	16,000
Instead of which a miller can now rent a windmill for about	2,000

He pays his man	1,000
Suppose he gains for his trouble and management	3,000
The same quantity of meal may therefore be produced for	6,000

instead of 16,000, which it would have cost if the process of the ancients had been still in use.

The same population is nevertheless fed; for the mill does not diminish the quantity of meal produced; the profits gained in society still suffice to pay for the new produce; for as soon as the 6000 francs are paid for expenses of production, that moment 6000 francs are gained in profit; and society enjoys this essential advantage, that the individuals of whom it consists, whatever be their means of existence, their incomes—whether they live by their labour, their capitals, or their landed possessions, reduce the portion of their expenses devoted to paying for the making of meal, in the proportion of sixteen to six, or by five-eights. Where a man must formerly have expended eight francs a year for this purpose, he will now have to lay out only three, which is exactly equivalent to an increase of income: for the five francs saved in this article may be spent on any other. If equal improvements took place in every article of produce in which we expend our incomes, those incomes would actually have been increased by five-eights; and a man who gets 3000 francs a year, whether by grinding corn, or in any other manner, would really be as rich as if he had gained 8000 before these improvements were made.

These considerations must have escaped the attention of M. *Sismondi,* when he wrote the following passage:—"* Whenever the demand for consumption exceeds the means of producing, every new discovery in mechanics or the arts is a benefit to society, because it furnishes the means of satisfying existing wants. But when the production is fully equal to the consumption, every such discovery is a calamity, because it only adds to the enjoyments of the consumers the opportunity of obtaining them at a cheaper rate, while it deprives the producers even of life itself. It would be odious to weigh the value of cheapness against that of existence."

It is plain that M. *Sismondi* does not adequately appreciate the advantages of cheapness, or conceive that what is saved in the expense of one article, may be laid out in additional purchases of another commodity, beginning with the most indispensable.

Hitherto no inconvenience has been known to arise from the invention of corn-mills; and their beneficial operation is seen in the diminished price of produce, which is equivalent to an increase of income to all those who make use of the invention.

But it is said that this increase of income obtained by the consumers, is taken from the profits of the nineteen unfortunate persons whom the mill has deprived of employment. This I deny. The nineteen labourers retain the possession of their industrious faculties, with the same strength, the same capacity, the same means of working, as before. The mill does not place them under the necessity of remaining without occupation, but only of finding another employment. Many circumstances are attended with this inconvenience, without producing similar advantages to compensate for it. A fashion which passes away, a war which closes a market, a change in the course of commerce, are a hundred times more ruinous to the labouring class than any new invention whatever.

It may still be insisted that, supposing the nineteen discarded labourers were instantly to find capitals to set them to work in some new branch of industry, they would not be able to sell their produce, because the mass of the productions of the society would be thereby increased, while the sum of its revenues would remain without addition. Is it then forgotten that the revenues of the society are increased by the very circumstance that there are nineteen new labourers? The wages of their labour form a revenue which enables them to acquire the produce of their labour, or to exchange it for any other equivalent commodities. This is sufficiently established by my preceding letters.

Strictly speaking, then, one disadvantage only remains—the necessity for these men to find a new occupation. Now the progress which is made in a particular department of industry, is favourable to industry in general. The increase of income which is derived from a saving in the expense of one article of consumption, tends to an expenditure on other objects. Nineteen men accustomed to grind corn have been deprived of that employment alone; a hundred new occupations, or extensions of the old branches of industry, have been thrown open to their exertions. I desire no better proof of this than the increase which has taken place in the works and population of every place in which the arts have attained a high degree of cultivation. We are so much accustomed to see the productions of new arts, that we scarcely remark them; but how forcibly would they strike the ancient inhabitants of Europe, could they revisit the earth! Let us imagine for a moment some, even of the most enlightened, such as Pliny or Archimedes, walking about one of our modern towns; they would think themselves surrounded by miracles. The abundance of our crystals and glasses, the magnitude and number of our mirrors, our clocks, our watches, the variety of our stuffs, our iron bridges, our engines of war, our ships, would astonish them beyond expression. And if they were to visit our workshops, what a multitude of occupations of which they could not have the least idea! Would they ever imagine that thirty thousand men are constantly employed all night, in Europe, in printing newspapers which people read the next morning while they are taking tea, coffee, chocolate, and other refreshments, as new to them as the newspapers themselves? Doubt not, Sir, that if the arts, as I find pleasure in thinking they will, continue to improve; that is to say, to produce more at less cost, new millions of men will, in a few ages, produce things which, could we rise up to see them, would excite in our minds no less surprise than Archimedes and Pliny would feel if they were to revive amongst us. We who scribble paper in search of truth, must be on our guard: if our writings should go down to our grandchildren, the terror with which we contemplate improvements which they will have greatly excelled, may probably appear to them somewhat laughable. And as to the workmen of your country, at once so ingenious and so miserable, our descendants may, perhaps, look upon them as persons, who were forced, in order to get their livelihood, to dance upon a rope with a weight fastened to their feet. They will read in history that some new plan was every day proposed to enable them to continue dancing, but unluckily the only one which could have been efficacious was omitted—the simple expedient of taking off the weight. Then our descendants, after having laughed at, may, perhaps, see reason to pity us.

I have said that beneficial improvements may be attended with transient inconveniences. Those which are produced by the invention of expeditious methods, are fortunately mitigated by circumstances which have been already described, and by others to which I have not yet alluded. It has been said that the cheapness resulting from an economical process, promotes the consumption of the article produced in such a manner, that a greater number of people are employed in its production than before; as has been observed in the spinning and weaving of cotton: and you yourself consider this circumstance alone as capable of more than compensating for the injury. I will add, that in proportion as machines and accelerating methods become more numerous, the difficulty of still discovering new improvements is increased; particularly in an old art in which the workmen are already formed. The most simple machines were first invented; afterwards came others more complex; but as they grow more complex, they are more expensive to establish, and require more human labour in their formation, which, in some degree, indemnifies the labouring classes for the work which they lose through the use of the new machine. The complication and dearness of a machine are obstacles to its being too suddenly adopted. The machine for dressing cloth by means of a rotary movement, cost, originally from 25,000 to 30,000 francs. Many manufacturers were at first unable to lay out such a sum; others hesitated, and still hesitate to adopt it, waiting for a satisfactory confirmation of its success. When machines are thus slowly introduced, almost all the inconveniences of such inventions are avoided. In short, I have always found, practically, that new machines produce more alarm than injury. As to the benefit arising from them, it is constant and durable.

M. de *Sismondi* raises an objection founded on what would happen supposing a hundred thousand knitters to make with their needles ten million pair of stockings, and a thousand workmen with stocking-frames to produce the same quantity. The result, according to him, would be, that the consumers of the stockings would only save fifty *centimes* (or half a franc) per pair, and yet that a manufacture which formerly maintained a hundred thousand persons, would now support only twelve hundred. But he obtains this result only by suppositions which are inadmissible.

To prove that the consumers of stockings would only pay fifty *centimes* less than before, he supposes that the costs of production would be, in the first case, as follows:—

10	millions for the purchase of the materials.
40	millions for the wages of 100,000 knitters at 400 francs each.
50	millions of francs, of which 40 millions would be distributed amongst the working manufacturers.

And in the second case, he sets down the expenses thus:

10	millions for the materials.
30	millions for the interest of the capital sunk, and profits of the proprietors.
2	millions for the interest of the circulating capital.
2	millions for repairs and renovation of machines.
1	million for the pay of 1200 workmen.
45	millions; of which one only would be devoted to the labouring class, instead of forty.

Now I observe in this account thirty millions for the interest of capital sunk, and the profit of the proprietors; which is to suppose a capital of two hundred millions for an undertaking capable of supporting twelve hundred men, and paying fifteen per cent for capital: a supposition truly extravagant.

A workman cannot use two frames at once; a thousand workmen would therefore require a thousand frames. A good stocking-frame costs six hundred francs; the thousand would consequently cost six hundred thousand francs. Add to this capital, a like capital for other utensils, workshops, &c., still the capital required will be only twelve hundred thousand francs. Admit that the interest and profits of the proprietors should be fifteen per cent on this capital, which is very fair; for a permanent business, which should produce more, would be reduced by competition to this rate of profit. This being allowed, we shall find for interest and profits of the proprietors one hundred and eighty thousand francs, instead of thirty millions.

A like observation applies to the two millions for the expenses of repairs, &c.; for even if new machines were to be bought every year instead of repairing the old ones, still they would only cost six hundred thousand francs. Nor would the circulating capital cost any think like two millions; for of what is this sum composed, according to M. *Sismondi*'s hypothesis? Of the raw materials, which he estimates at ten millions, and the wages, for which he allows one million; altogether eleven millions: the interest whereof at five per cent is five hundred and fifty thousand francs. But as in this business the manufactures may be completed and sold in less than six months, the capital, for which interest is to be allowed for the year, may be employed twice, and would cost each time only two hundred and seventy-five thousand francs, instead of two millions.

All these expenses together make only twelve millions fifty-five thousand francs, instead of fifty millions, which, according to M. de *Sismondi*'s suppositions, would be the cost of the stockings made by the knitting-needles. I am far from supposing that the saving would be so enormous, for while the author has greatly exaggerated the capital requisite for the machines, he has attributed to them too great a degree of efficacy in supposing they would enable twelve hundred workmen to do the work of a hundred thousand; but I say, that if the saving in this production were really so great, the low price of the stockings, or any other article of clothing produced under similar circumstances, would operate so favourably in extending the consumption, that instead of the hundred thousand supposed workmen being reduced to twelve hundred, their number would, in all probability, be doubled.

And if the consumption of this particular article would not admit of so excessive a multiplication of the same commodity, the demand for other kinds of produce would be increased in proportion; for observe, that after the introduction of the machines, society retains the same revenues as before; that is to say, the same number of workmen, the same amount of capital, the same land. Now, if instead of devoting, out of this mass of revenue, fifty millions to the purchase of stockings, the introduction of the frames should make it no longer necessary to lay out more than twelve in this article, the thirty-eight millions remaining would be applicable to the purchase of other articles of consumption, if not to the extended consumption of the same.

These arguments we learn from principles, and they are confirmed by experience. The distress endured by the population of England, which M. de *Sismondi* laments with the feeling of a true philanthropist, originates in other causes: it is chiefly caused by the *poor laws* of that country; and, as I have before observed, by a mass of taxes, which renders production too expensive; so that, when goods are offered for sale, the incomes of a great proportion of consumers are insufficient to enable them to pay the prices which the manufacturer or producer is absolutely compelled to demand.

Notes

[*] "When a machine is invented, which, by saving labour, will bring goods into the market at a much cheaper rate than before, the most usual effort is such an extension of the demand for the commodity, that the value of the whole mass of goods made by the new machinery greatly exceeds their former value; and notwithstanding the saving of labour, more hands instead of fewer, are required in the manufacture.—P. 402.

"But we must allow that the preeminent advantages derived from the substitution of machinery for manual labour, depend upon the extension of the market for the commodities produced, and the increased stimulus given to consumption; and that, without this extension of market, and increase of consumption, they must be in a great degree lost." —P. 412.

[*] Nouveaux Principes, &c. tom. ii. p. 317.

LETTER V.

Sir,

On reading your *Principles of Political Economy*, the first object which excited my attention, was that great malady which at present afflicts mankind, and which prevents their living upon their productions. Although in the order of things, a discussion on the nature of riches ought to precede it, to assist the mind in comprehending all the phenomena which relate to their formation and distribution; I did not think it necessary to give it precedence, because it appeared more especially to interest those only who cultivate political economy as a science, and without any view to practical application. However, I cannot lay down my pen without giving you my opinion on this point. You authorize me to do this by the noble frankness with which you invite discussions which may enlighten the public. "It is extremely desirable," you say (p. 4), "that those who are considered by the public the most competent judges, should agree on the principal propositions." We cannot therefore make them too plain.

You object to the definition which Lord *Lauderdale* gives of riches when he says that they are *all that man desires as being useful or agreeable to him*, as too vague; and I think you have great reason. I look for that which you think ought to be substituted for it; and I find that you give the name of riches to all the *material* objects which are necessary, useful, or agreeable to man (p. 28). The only difference which I observe between these two definitions consists in the word *material* which you add to that of Lord *Lauderdale;* and I confess this word appears to me any thing but the truth.

You must be aware of my reasons. The great discovery of political economy, that which will ever render it invaluable, is the having shewn that every thing is convertible into riches. Man has learnt from thence how he must conduct himself to possess the happy means of satisfying his desires. But, as I have already had occasion to observe, it is beyond the power of man, to add a single atom to the mass of matter of which the world is composed. If he then creates riches, riches are not material: there is no middle point. Man can only, by means of his capital and his lands, change the combinations of matter, and thus make it useful to him; but utility is an *immaterial* quality.

This is not all, Sir. I fear that your definition does not comprise the essential quality of riches. Permit me to explain.

Adam Smith, as well as every body else, has remarked that a glass of water, which may be a very desirable thing when one is dry, is not riches. It is, however, a *material* object, it is necessary, useful, and agreeable to man. It possesses all the conditions of your definition: but yet it is not riches. It is not that however which is the subject of our investigation and the matter of your book. What does it require to become so? — to have value.

There are then things which are natural riches, which are most precious to man; but are not such riches as political economy can interfere with. Can they be increased? Can they be consumed? No: they are regulated by other laws than those of political economy. A glass of water is subject to the laws of natural philosophy; the attachment of our friends and our reputation in the world are governed by the moral law; but are not within the compass of political economy. Which then are the riches within the jurisdiction of that science? — Those which are susceptible of creation and destruction, of *more* and of *less;* and what, I again ask, is this *more,* this *less,* but value?

You are yourself, Sir, compelled to admit this in many places. You say (p. 340), "It appears then that the wealth of a country depends partly upon the quantity of produce obtained by its labour" (it depends entirely upon it), "and partly upon such an adaptation of it to the wants and power of the exerting population as is calculated to give it value." And in the following page you are still more positive. After having advanced further into the discussion, you confess that "it is obvious that, in the actual state of things, the value of commodities - - - - may be said to be the sole cause of the existence of wealth." How then has it happened that a condition so essential as *value* has been left out of your definition?

But this is not sufficient. The nature of riches will be very imperfectly known to us if we are not able to fix some precise meaning to this word *value*. In order to be possessed of great wealth will it be enough that we estimate at a high rate the goods we possess? If I build a house, with which I am delighted, and which I choose to estimate at ten thousand pounds, does this house make me really worth ten thousand pounds? We receive a present from one who is dear to us; it is inestimable in our eyes; does it follow that it has made us immensely rich? You cannot think so. In order to constitute riches, the value must be *recognised,* not by the possessor merely, but by other persons. But what more irrefragable proof that its value is *recognised* can be given than that other persons are ready to give for it a certain quantity of other things which are valuable. Notwithstanding the value of ten thousand pounds which I set upon my house, yet if I cannot find any body who will give me more than five thousand pounds for it, I cannot say that it is worth ten thousand pounds: it is really worth no more than five thousand pounds; it will produce me no greater amount than five thousand pounds, or whatever value may be had for that sum.

Adam Smith also (b. i. c.4) immediately after having observed that there are two kinds of value, and having, very improperly in my opinion, called one of them *value in use,* and the other *value in exchange,* abandons entirely the former, and is solely occupied throughout his work with *exchangeable value.* This is what you have done yourself, Sir;* what Mr. *Ricardo* has done; what I have done; what all of us have done; for the plain reason, that there is no other value in political economy; that that alone is subject to fixed laws; that that alone can be created, distributed, and destroyed, according to rules which are invariable, and which are capable of becoming an object of scientific inquiry. It is a necessary consequence, the price of every thing being its *exchangeable* value estimated in money, that there is no other price in political economy than *market price:* that that which *Smith* calls the *natural price,* is no more natural than any other;

it is the cost of production; it is the market price of productive services.

I will not deny, Sir, that you have, in Mr. Ricardo, a powerful and respectable ally. He is against you in the subject of *markets,* and fights on your side in the question of *value;* but notwithstanding my connexion with him, and the reciprocal esteem we bear for each other, I have not hesitated to combat his arguments:† the first object of both of us, and of you too, Sir, I am sure, is the love of truth, and the happiness of mankind.

These are Mr. Ricardo's words: (2d edit. c. 20) "Value differs essentially from riches; for value does not depend on the abundance (of things necessary or agreeable) but on the difficulty or facility of their production. The labour of a million of men in manufactories will always produce the same value, but not the same riches. By the invention of machinery, by improvement in skill, by a better division of labour, or by the discovery of new markets, where more advantageous exchanges may be made, a million of men may produce double or treble the amount of riches, of *necessaries, conveniences, and amusements,* in one state of society, that they could produce in another; but they will not on that account add any thing to value." (c. 20. 2d. edit.)

This argument, founded on facts which are not contested, appears to accord perfectly with the opinions you maintain. The question whether these facts confirm or destroy that doctrine of value which teaches that riches are composed of the value of the things we possess, applying the word *value* to those values only which are recognized and exchangeable. What is there, in fact, but value, but that quality capable of appreciation, capable of being *more* or *less,* which exists in the things we possess? It is the quality which enables us to obtain, in exchange for the things we have, those of which we are in want. This value is so much the greater, as the thing we have will procure a greater quantity of the thing we want. Thus if I desire to exchange a horse which I possess, for corn that I want; that is to say, if I desire to sell my horse to buy corn, if my horse is worth sixty pounds, I have twice as much value to convert into corn as if my horse was only worth thirty pounds: I should have twice as many bushels of corn, and this portion of my property will be twice as great. And as the same reasoning may be applied generally to all that I possess, it follows that our riches must be measured by the value of the things we possess. This is a consequence that none can reasonably dispute.

You cannot deny, says Mr. Ricardo to me, that we are the *more* rich, the *more* agreeable and necessary things we have to consume, *whatever may otherwise be their value.* I do not deny it: but have we not more things to consume when we have the power of acquiring them in greater quantity? To have in one's hands the power of purchasing a greater quantity of useful things, a greater *quantity of utility,* extending this expression to whatever is necessary and agreeable, is to possess *more* riches. But this proposition does not contradict whatever there is of truth in the definition of riches given by Mr. *Ricardo* and yourself. You say that riches consists in the quantity of necessary and agreeable things we possess. I say so too; but these words, *quantity of things necessary and agreeable,* have a very vague and arbitrary meaning, unfit to enter into a perfect definition: I render them precise and clear by the idea of their *exchangeable value.* The condition of *utility* then is the being equal to another utility, which men are willing to give in exchange for that which you possess. It becomes then an *equation.* We can compare one with another by means of a third. A sack of corn is equal in value to a piece of stuff, when each of them can be exchanged for the same number of shillings. This then serves as a basis for all comparisons; what enables us to measure an increase, or a diminution; in a word, this is the foundation of a science. Political economy is nothing without it: it is this consideration alone which has taken it out of the dominion of fancy; it is so essential that you have been compelled to do homage to it yourself without intending it; and that there is not one of your arguments in which it is not either expressed or understood. If it had not been so, you would have caused the science to retrograde, instead of enriching it with new truths.

While your definition, and that of Mr. *Ricardo,* is wanting in precision, it is also wanting in extent: it does not embrace the whole of what constitutes our riches. What! are our riches limited to objects which are *material,* necessary, and agreeable? What then do you think of our talents? Do they not belong to the productive powers? Do we not draw revenues from them? Revenues more or less large, in the same manner as we draw a greater revenue from an acre of good land than from an acre of heath? I know some admirable artists who have no other income than what they derive from their talents, and who yet live in opulence. According to you, they ought to be no richer than a dauber of signs.

It is impossible for you to deny, that whatever has an exchangeable value makes part of our wealth. It is composed entirely of the productive powers which we possess; our lands, our capitals, and our personal faculties. Of these, land is alienable, but not consumable—capital is both alienable and consumable; while talents, though incapable of alienation, are consumable; they perish with those who possess them. From these funds, all the revenues upon which society subsists are derived; and (what may appear paradoxical, although it is perfectly true) all these revenues are *immaterial;* for they are derived from an immaterial quality—*utility.* The different kinds of utility are derived from our productive powers, and are comparable with each other by their value, which I have no need here to denominate *exchangeable,* because I can not recognize any value in political economy which is not exchangeable.

As to the difficulty raised by Mr. *Ricardo,* that by improved processes a million of people might produce twice or thrice as much riches, without producing more values, it vanishes when we consider, as we ought, production as an exchange in which the *productive services* of labour, land, and capital is *given,* in order to *obtain* the *production.* It is by means of these services that we obtain all the productions which exists in the world; and this, by the bye, is what gives value to productions; for after having acquired them by dint of labour or expense, we do not part from them for nothing. Now, since our first *riches* are the productive powers we possess, and our first *revenues* are the productive services which emanate from them, we are so much the richer; our productive services have so much the greater value, as they may be able to obtain in the exchange called *production,* a *greater quantity* of useful things. And as a *greater quantity of useful things,* and their *greater cheapness,* are expressions perfectly synonymous, the producers are richer when productions are more abundant, and less dear. I say the producers generally, because competition compels them to give their productions for what they have cost;* so that when the producers of corn or stuffs have succeeded, with the same quantity of productive services, to produce twice the quantity of corn or stuff, all other producers will be able to purchase double the quantity of corn or stuff with the same quantity of productive services, or, which is the same thing, with the productions which result from them.

This, Sir, is the well-founded doctrine, without which I consider it impossible to explain the very great difficulties of political economy, and particularly how it is that a nation can become richer while its productions diminish in value, although riches consist in value. You see that I do not fear to lay down my pretended paradoxes in their simplest form. I strip them completely naked, and submit them to the candour of Mr. *Ricardo* and yourself, and to the good sense of the public. I shall however hold myself at liberty to explain them if they are misunderstood, and to defend them with perseverance if they are unjustly attacked.

Notes

[*] "It is obviously therefore the value of commodities, or" (that is to say) "*the sacrifice of labour, and of other articles which people are willing to make in order to obtain them*" *in exchange,* &c. p. 341.

[†] In notes which I have added to the French translation of Mr. Ricardo's *Principles of Political Economy.*

[*] It is always to be remembered that the profits of the manufacturer are considered as part of the cost, or charges of production. — Tr.

THE END.

ADVERTISEMENT.

This Work does not pretend to furnish the means of becoming rich: it professes only to point them out. Wealth cannot be produced from nothing, but a clock may be made with wheels; and, as men may be taught to make a clock, so they may be taught to make what is called Riches.

Many men have the materials within their reach who do not suspect it; and as for those who have them not, is it useless even to them to know where they are to be found, and how they may be employed?

Some men may be better able than others to profit by the perusal of this little Work; but I venture to assert, that there is no person who may not derive from it some advantage.

It has been asked, why I did not publish this Catechism, as being more elementary, before my *"Traité d'Economie Politique."* The reason is evident. If I had not previously proved in a work of detail, by numerous examples and strict reasoning, that Political Economy, in the present state of the science, is only the exposition of what is passing every day; and that all the facts are so intimately connected together, that it has become easy to refer to their causes, and to deduce from them satisfactory results, every thing must have been taken upon my credit; and I am far from pretending to so much deference.

An elementary work is necessarily somewhat dogmatical. But when truths are not promulgated under the sanction of an acknowledged authority, it is not only necessary to be in the right, but to prove that one is so. And how could these proofs have been established in so small a compass, and at the same time have been rendered intelligible to the uninformed?

This task is however no longer requisite, as the proofs of every thing, which might appear to be mere assertion, are to be found in a more extensive work, which has been adopted by foreigners as well as the

French, and strengthened by the approbation of men, the most versed, in Europe, in the practice as well as the theory of Values.

Those who possess the most elevated minds have generally most goodness of heart. They will feel what a happy influence the true principles of Political Economy, better understood, are capable of exerting on the lot of mankind; and perhaps they will judge, that my efforts to spread them are not unworthy of their sanction.

J. B. SAY.

CATECHISM OF POLITICAL ECONOMY; OR, FAMILIAR CONVERSATIONS ON THE MANNER IN WHICH WEALTH IS PRODUCED, DISTRIBUTED, AND CONSUMED.

CHAPTER THE FIRST.
ON THE COMPOSITION OF WEALTH AND THE USE OF MONEY.

What do you understand by the word wealth?

Whatever has a value; gold, silver, land, merchandise . . . . .

Are not gold and silver preferable to other wealth?

That is preferable in which the greatest value is to be found. One hundred and ten guineas in corn are preferable to one hundred guineas in gold.

But, where the value is equal, is not the money better than the merchandise?

In fact, it is preferred.

What is the reason of it?

The custom generally established of using money as a medium in exchanges, renders that species of merchandise more convenient than any other for those who have purchases to make; that is, for every body.

What do you mean by money being a medium of exchanges?

If you are a farmer and desire to exchange a part of your corn for cloth, you begin by procuring money for your corn; then with that money you buy cloth.

Without doubt.

76

You have in reality made a double exchange, in which you have given corn to one man, and another has given cloth to you.

That is true.

The value of this corn was transitorily in money, afterwards in cloth; and though you have in fact exchanged your corn for cloth, money was the *intermediate* form which that value assumed in order to change itself into cloth. Such is the use of money.

Well! But if all these values are equal, why is that of money preferred?

Because, when a man once possesses money, he need make only one exchange, in order to obtain what he may want; while he who possesses every other merchandise, has two exchanges to make. He must, in the first place, exchange his merchandise for money, and afterwards his money for merchandise.

Can you make use of any other thing for this purpose instead of money?

Yes; there are countries in which shells and other articles are used; but the metals, and principally gold and silver, are of all materials, the most convenient to be used as money. It is that which has caused them to be adopted by all civilized and commercial nations.

Then in those countries in which shells are used as money, they are the objects which, the value being equal, are preferred in exchanges?

They are so in effect: but the precious metals are more sought after than the other monies, because they possess, as merchandise, certain advantages which increase the preference they possess as money. They contain much value in small bulk, which permits them to be easily concealed and carried from place to place; they do not spoil by keeping; they may be divided or reunited at will, almost without loss; in fine, they are valuable all over the world, and whatever frequented place we travel to with this sort of wealth, we are sure, on more or less favourable conditions, to be able to exchange it for whatever we may want.

I comprehend the reason why money, and, above all, money of gold and silver, is more desirable than any other merchandise; but how can we procure it?

As we procure every thing else that we want, by an exchange when we have not a mine that produces it; in the same way that we procure fruit when we do not possess the tree that bears it.

How can we obtain a thing in order to give it in exchange for money?

Produce it.

Produce a thing! But supposing that possible, how shall I be certain that I shall get money for that thing?

You may assure yourself of that by giving it a value.

But how can a value be given to things?

We shall see that in the following chapters.

CHAPTER II.
ON THE UTILITY AND VALUE OF PRODUCTS.

What do you understand by the word Products?

I understand all those things to which men have consented to give a value.

How is value given to a thing?

By giving it utility.

How is the utility of a thing the cause of its having a value?

Because persons are then to be found who are in want of this thing; they desire to have it from those who produce it. These, on their side, will not part from it until they are paid the expenses they have been at in producing it, including their profits. The value of the thing is established by the result of this opposition between the producer and the consumer.

But there are many things of great utility, and no value, as water. Why have they no value?

Because nature gives them gratuitously, and without stint, and we are not obliged to produce them. If a person was able to create water, and wished to sell it, no one would buy it, because it could be got at the river for nothing. Thus all the world enjoy these things, but they are not riches to any body. If all things that men could desire were in the same case, no one would be rich, but no one would be in want of riches, since each could enjoy all things at his pleasure.

But this is not the case: the greater part of things which are necessary and even indispensible to us, are not given to us gratuitously and unlimitedly. Human industry must, with pains and labour, collect, fashion and transport them.

They then become *products*. The utility, the faculty they have acquired of being serviceable, gives them a value and this value is *riches*.

When once riches are thus created they may be exchanged for other riches, other values, and we may procure the products which we want in exchange for those we can spare. We have seen in the preceding chapter how money facilitates this exchange.

I now conceive how products alone are riches; but their utility does not appear to be the only cause which gives them value; for there are products, such as rings and artificial flowers, which have value but no utility.

You do not discover the utility of these products because you call only *useful* that which is so to the eye of reason, but you ought to understand by that word whatever is capable of satisfying the wants and desires of man such as he is. His vanity and his passions are to him wants, sometimes as imperious as hunger. He is the sole judge of the importance that things are of to him, and of the want he has of them. We cannot judge of it but by the price he puts on them. The value of things is the sole measure of their utility to man. It is enough for us to give them utility *in his eyes* in order to give them a value. Now that is what we call *to produce*, to create products.

Recapitulate what you have said.

Give to any thing, to a material which has no value, *utility*, and you give it a *value*; that is, you make a *product* of it, you create *wealth*.

One can then create wealth?

Incontestibly.

I thought that man could not create any thing.

He cannot create matter: he cannot make the laws which regulate nature; but with existing matter and the laws of nature such as they are, he can give a value to certain things, and consequently can create wealth.

What country may be called a rich country?

One in which many things of value, or more briefly, many values are to be found; in the same manner as a family which possesses many of these values is a rich family.

CHAPTER III.
ON PRODUCTION.

You have told me that to produce *is to give utility to things: how is* utility *given? How are we to* produce?

In an infinity of ways; but for our convenience we may arrange, in three classes, every manner of producing.

What is the first manner of producing?

It consists in *collecting or gathering together* those things which nature creates, either without the intervention of man, such as fish and minerals; or, such as men have, by the cultivation of the earth, and by means of seeds, induced and assisted nature to produce. All these works are alike in their object. They are called *Agricultural Industry.*

What utility is given to a thing by him who finds it ready made to his hands; as the fisherman who takes a fish, or the miner who collects minerals?

He renders it fit for use. The fish, while it is in the sea, is useless. As soon as it is brought to the market we can make use of it. In like manner, it is in vain that coal exists in the bosom of the earth; while there, it is of no utility; it neither warms us, nor heats the iron in the forge: it is the industry of the miner that makes it fit for these purposes. He creates, by extracting it from the earth, all the value that it has when extracted.

How does the cultivator create value?

The materials, of which a sack of corn is composed, are not drawn from nothing; they existed before the corn was corn: they were diffused through the earth, the water, and the air, and had no value whatever. The industry of the cultivator, in taking measures to bring these different matters together, first under the form of grain, and afterwards of a sack of corn, created a value which they had not before. It is the same with all the other products of agriculture.

What is the second manner of producing?

It consists in giving to the product of another industry a greater value, by the new forms which we give to it, by the changes which it is made to undergo. The miner procures the metal of which a buckle is made; but a buckle, when made, is worth more than the metal of which it is formed. The value of the buckle above that of the metal is a value produced, and the buckle is the product of two kinds of industry: of that of the miner, and that of the manufacturer. This last is called *manufacturing industry.*

What works are included in manufacturing industry?

It includes the most ordinary as well as the most exquisite workmanship, the form given by a rough village artisan to a pair of wooden shoes, as well as that given to a piece of jewellery. It includes alike the work executed by a single cobler in his stall, and by hundreds of workmen in a vast manufactory.

What is the third manner of producing?

We produce also by buying a product in one place, where it is of a less value, and conveying it to another, where it is of greater value. This is the work of *Commercial Industry.*

How does commercial industry produce utility, as it neither changes the form nor the substance of a product, which is sold just as it is bought?

It acts like the fisherman, of whom we have just spoken; it takes a product from a place where it cannot be used; from a place, at least, where its uses are less extensive, less precious, to a place where they are more so, or where its production is less easy, less abundant, and dearer. Wood is little used, and consequently of very limited utility in the mountains, where it so far exceeds the wants of the inhabitants, that it is sometimes left to rot; this utility,* however, becomes very considerable when the same wood is transported into a city. Hides are of little value in South America, where they have a great number of wild animals: the same skins have a great value in Europe, where their production is expensive, and their uses much more multiplied. Commercial Industry, in bringing them, augments their value by all the difference between their price in Brazil and their price in Europe.

What is comprehended under the term Commercial Industry?

Every species of industry which takes a product from one place and transports it to another, where it is more precious, and which thus brings it within the reach of those who want it. It includes also, by analogy, the industry which, by retailing a product, brings it within the reach of small consumers. Thus the grocer, who buys merchandise in gross to resell it in detail in the same town; and the butcher, who buys whole beasts to resell them piece by piece, exercises *Commercial Industry.*

Is there not great similarity between these different modes of producing?

The greatest. They all consist in taking a product in one state, and delivering it in another, in which it has a greater utility and a higher value. They may be all reduced to one species. If we distinguish them here, it is to facilitate the study of their results, but notwithstanding all our distinctions it is often very difficult to separate one kind of industry from another. A villager, who makes baskets, is a manufacturer; when he carries them to market, he becomes commercial. But no matter by which means, the moment that we create or that we augment the utility of things, we augment their value, we exercise an industry, we produce wealth.

For shortness, Agricultural Industry may be called *Agriculture;* Manufacturing Industry may be called *Manufactures;* and Commercial Industry, *Commerce.*

Notes

[*] We must never forget that, by the words *utility of things,* we mean the faculty they have of serving those purposes, to which man thinks proper to apply them.

CHAPTER IV.
ON THE OPERATIONS COMMON TO ALL THE SPECIES OF INDUSTRY.

I have just seen that agriculture, manufactures, and commerce are productive of wealth: by what means do they attain that end?

An industrious undertaking, whatever it may be, is an enterprize in which a man decides, what part of the material and of the laws of the physical and moral world he is able to apply to the production of a useful thing.

What do you understand by the laws of the physical world?

I understand the laws to which material beings are subjected; thus, metals are softened by heat: this is a physical law.

Give me an example of the use of this physical law in any industrious enterprize?

A blacksmith, who uses heat to soften a piece of iron of which he makes a horse-shoe, is the undertaker of a manufacturing industry, who avails himself of that physical law; in the same manner, the merchant, who fits out a vessel, uses for the purpose of sending it beyond seas, the power of the winds, which are themselves the effects of some other law of the physical world.

What do you understand by the laws of the moral world?

They are the rules to which we are subjected by the customs, the wants, and the will of mankind.

Give me an instance in which the undertaker of any industry consults the laws of the moral world?

He consults them when he informs himself of the manners, the wants, and the legislation of men, which may either enable him to procure the materials for his industry, or furnish him with consumers of his products. Some of these laws belong to the nature of man, others to the manners of the country and age in which we live. He who takes into his calculation human vanity, runs little risk of deceiving himself. A hatter who carries on, in a proper manner, his business among us, has a lucrative occupation. He would have gained nothing among the ancients, who did not wear hats.

Who are those who study the laws of the physical world?

Those who cultivate the physical and mathematical sciences: such as chemists, naturalists, geometricians, &c.

Who are those who study the laws of the moral world?

Those who inform themselves of morals, politics, history, geography, travels, &c.

I understand: the learned serve as guides to the industrious?

Just so: and the work of the one, as well as the other, is productive, since they concur in creating products. It is only in civilized and enlightened countries that we see a very great and productive industry. It is there only that we find that great mass of acquired knowledge, of which the industrious, the agriculturists, manufacturers, and merchants, avail themselves.

Are the learned, and the undertakers of works of industry, the only industrious men?

No. There are also workmen under the direction of the undertakers of works of industry. When a workman carries on an enterprize on his own account, as the knife-grinder in the streets, he is both workman and undertaker.

CHAPTER V.
ON CAPITAL AND LAND.

Is it sufficient for an undertaker of industry to have the talents and judgment which constitutes his industry?

No: his judgment and his talent would be exercised upon nothing. He must possess, besides those, the materials on which he would employ his industry, and the indispensible implements to carry it into effect. All these things have a value previously acquired, and this value is called *capital.*

I thought that capital was a sum of money, and not materials and utensils?

The value of a capital at the moment in which it is borrowed may have the form of money: but it has it only transitorily, in the same manner that the corn which a producer of corn desires to exchange for cloth, is exchanged in the first place for money, which is to be again exchanged for cloth.* The values which we save, in order to be employed as capitals are, in the same manner, products which we successively exchange for money, and when we desire to use them as capital, we exchange them again for products necessary to production.

You say that capital *is composed of products, that is to say, of things or values produced by the industry of man: a capital is then always a value which is moveable?*

No: the products of human industry may be either moveable or immoveable. A house is a product of human industry. In works of agriculture, besides the value of the land, which may be considered as a great and admirable instrument in the hands of man, and which, on this account, makes part of his capital, the clearings, the buildings, and the inclosures, which are improvements of this grand instrument, are products of industry.

Are there not also moveable values in the capital of an agriculturist?

88

Yes; the implements of labour, the cattle, the seed, as well as the provisions for his family, his servants, and his animals: and even the money that is destined for the outgoings which his undertaking requires.

Tell me of what the capital of a manufacturer; a weaver, for example, consists.

It is composed of the value of his first material, which may be either cotton, flax, wool, or silk: also of his looms, shuttles, and other implements: and, in fact, of every value which he is obliged to advance for his own maintenance as well as that of his workmen.

If the value of the capital is employed in the purchase of all these things, how is it that it is not lost?

Because the result of all these things is a ribband or a cloth, the value of which reimburses the capital, and pays besides to the weaver the profits of his industry. In the same manner, the capital of the merchant consists principally of the value of the merchandise in which he trades, and this merchandise, augmenting in value in his hands, represents at all times his capital increased by his profits.

How does a man, engaged in industry, know whether the value of his capital is increased or diminished?

By an inventory; that is, by a detailed account of all that he possesses, in which every thing is valued according to its current price.

Notes

[*] See Chapter I. on the Use of Money.

89

CHAPTER VI.
ON THE FORMATION OF CAPITAL.

I SEE that to create values, that is, riches, industrious talents and capital are necessary. I can conceive that industrious talents may be acquired by study and practice; but how is capital to be procured?

It must be created, or borrowed of those who have created it.

How can it be created?

To answer this question, it is necessary to begin by giving some notions on consumption, although this is not the proper place, and it ought to be developed hereafter.

What do you understand by consumption?

Consumption is the opposite of production: it is a destruction of values produced. We cannot destroy matter any more than we can create it; but we can destroy the utility that has been given to it; and, in destroying its utility, we destroy its value. That is what is called *"to consume."*

We do not wantonly destroy things of value: what end is proposed in doing so?

Either to procure an enjoyment or else to reproduce another value. The consumption of food or clothing is an enjoyment: it has no other result. *Reproductive consumption* is neither so simple nor so easy.

In what does it consist?

It consists in the industrious destruction of one value, so as to produce another in place of that which is destroyed, and which exceeds it in value sufficiently to pay for the industry employed in the operation. Thus the agriculturist who sows a grain of corn destroys the value of it, but he does not destroy it in the same manner as he who eats it: he destroys it in such manner as that it shall be reproduced with profit: and even if he employs this grain or many grains in feeding fowls, he still destroys the value of this grain; but as he increases the value of the fowls, he produces a value which usually replaces, with profit, the value which was consumed. This is called *reproductive consumption.*

Every thing that a man consumes for his own use is then an unproductive consumption?

No, not all. When eatables, drinkables, or wearing apparel, are consumed by men who are at the same time employed in producing a value equal, or superior, to what they consume, it becomes a *reproductive consumption.* It is so much the more reproductive as the value of the products which these men have created during the consumption exceeds the value of those they have consumed.

Give me examples of reproductive consumption drawn from manufacturing industry?

Besides the maintenance of his workmen and agents, a manufacturer consumes the materials which he transforms. He consumes, also, although more slowly, the utensils he employs. Thus a soap-maker consumes, reproductively, oil, soda, wood, or coal, cauldrons, &c. and even the place and workshops in which he exercises his industry.

Give me examples of reproductive consumption in commercial industry?

A merchant consumes the value of the maintenance of his workmen, that is, of his carriers, lightermen, sailors, porters, and agents of every sort: he consumes also his instruments, which are carts, horses, ships, warehouses; and we may even consider as part of his consumption, the advances which be makes for the purchase of his merchandise. All these advances are restored to him by the value of the products which go out of his hands: that is, the merchandise in a state to be sold.

All these undertakers of industry reproduce with loss, or without either loss or gain, or with profit, according as they reproduce values, which are either inferior, equal, or superior to the values which they have consumed.

What is the effect of these facts, as it respects capital?

That which is called *productive capital*, or, simply, *capital*, consists of all those values, or, if you will, all those advances employed reproductively, and replaced in proportion as they are destroyed.

It is easy to see that this term *capital* has no relation to the nature or form of the values of which capital is composed (their nature and form vary perpetually); but refers to the use, to the reproductive consumption of these values: thus a bushel of corn forms no part of my capital if I employ it to make cakes to treat my friends, but it does form part of my capital if I use it in maintaining workmen who are employed on the production of that which will repay me its value. In the same manner a sum of money is no longer a part of my capital if I exchange it for products which I consume: but it does form part of my capital if I exchange it for a value which is to remain and augment in my hands.

How is capital amassed?

Capital is augmented by all that is withdrawn from *unproductive* consumption, and added to a *consumption which is reproductive.*

Capitals that are amassed are then consumed?

Without doubt.

Can capitals be amassed without being consumed?

Yes, capitals, that is, values may be amassed under one form as well as another, in gold, silver, or merchandise, and no part of it used for production. These are idle capitals, which may become productive hereafter, but which in the mean time do not yield any of those profits which we shall consider presently. Capital thus accumulated may be transferred from one to another by exchange or by succession, and may be lent in one form as well as in another, either in the form of merchandise or of money: but in whatever form it is transferred or lent, it consists in the value of the things transferred or lent, and not in the things themselves. Thus when Paul a clothier sells cloaths on credit to Silvan a woollen draper, he really lends to Silvan the value for which he gives him credit; although this value is not lent in money, but in merchandise, and although it is to be returned not in merchandise but in money.

Is land a capital?

Land is made use of in the way of capital. It is an instrument for which no other can be substituted, and by means of which we make materials for our use, and consequently give them a value. It may be transmitted or lent (by way of letting) as capital may: but it differs from capital as it is not a human production, but is furnished to us by nature, and is incapable of increase by accumulation like capital.

I comprehend that a capital, which is a mass of values accumulated by the care which has been taken to snatch them successively from improductive, and to devote them to reproductive consumption, belongs to him who has taken the pains and imposed on himself the privations of which it is the fruit: but why should land, which is given gratuitously by nature, be the property of any one?

It is not the object of political economy to inquire what may have been the origin of the right to property. It shews only that land, and consequently its products, is susceptible of appropriation, that is to say, of becoming the exclusive property of such or such; and that this appropriation is highly favourable to production: for if land and the products to be derived from it, did not belong exclusively to some one, no one would take the pains, nor make the advances necessary, to obtain these products; much less to cultivate and enrich the soil. For the same reason it is useful that capital and its products should be an exclusive property; it is the only means of inducing its accumulation and its productive employment.

You have said that land differs from capital, inasmuch as it is not like the latter, capable of extension; but the clearing, the buildings and the enclosures by increasing the products, are equivalent to an actual extension.

The improvements which are values accumulated by industry on land are a capital, and the profits which result from the whole are the united profits of capital and land.

But how can we transfer or lend capital of this kind?

It can only be done by transferring or lending at the same time the land itself. It is for this reason that capital so employed is called an *appropriated capital.* There is in the same manner much capital locked up in many manufactories, in all the utensils and in the buildings which are generally much more valuable than the land on which they stand. Thus when we have exchanged a moveable capital for a mill, a forge or a house to live in, we cannot put ourselves again into the possession of that portion of our capital, without selling at the same time the land as well as the buildings upon it.

The other capital is called *circulating capital.* There is no other difference between them than that the materials of which these respective capitals are composed, are more conveniently and more easily exchanged, and in smaller portions in the one case than in the other.

CHAPTER VII.
ON THE MANNER IN WHICH THE VALUE OF PRODUCTS IS ESTABLISHED, AND OF THE CHARGES OF PRODUCTION.

We have seen how utility is given to things: we have seen that utility gives them value; how is that value fixed, the amount of which constitutes riches?

The utility which the things have acquired, causes them to be sought after, to be wanted; a price is offered for them; and when this price is sufficient to defray the expenses which their production would cost, they will be produced.

Of what are the expenses of production composed?

Of whatever must be paid to obtain the co-operation of the agents of production.

What are the agents of production?

They are the means indispensably necessary for the creation of a product: viz. *human industry;* the *capital* or value which serves for that purpose; the *land* and other natural agents which contribute to it.

To whom do you give the name of producers?

To all those who possess any of the agents of production. A man who exercises an industry, and the possessor of capital or of land are *producers*.

Why do you call the possessors of capital or of land, producers, even when they do not labour themselves?

Because the capital and the land, concurring in the formation of products, those who furnish these means of production contribute to it effectually themselves.

What do you say of him who employs his own capital or cultivates his own land?

That he contributes doubly: first, by his industry; afterwards as a capitalist or landholder: but although these functions are often filled by one person, it is convenient to separate them when they are to be studied, in order to distinguish properly what belongs to each species of productive service.

What is meant by the term productive service?

It is the service rendered by each of the agents of production: the service rendered by industry; the service rendered by capital, and the service rendered by natural agents.

I see what is the cause of the demand and of the payment for productive services: what is it that limits this demand?

The property of the consumers, or of those who desire to use the product. There would be no bounds to the demand for any useful thing if it was not to be paid for. There is no other effective demand than that which is accompanied by the offer of a price: and it is this price which in paying for the product pays at the same time for the services which were necessary to its production.

What happens when the price of the product is not sufficient to pay the charges of production?

Then the producers will not exchange their productive services for the price of the product; and the production does not take place.

What happens when the price of the product is more than enough to pay the charges of production?

The producers of this kind of product become more numerous, and their competition will cause the price of the product to fall.

Can one let out or lend productive services?

Yes, when a man lets out his industry, the price which is paid for it is called *wages*. When he lets out his capital it is called *interest*. When he lets out his land, the tenant is called a *farmer*, and the price is called *rent*.

What do you understand by letting out industry?

It is to give for hire time, talent, and labour; to co-operate in the creation of a product of industry.

Who is it that hires the labour of the one, the capital or the land of the others?

It is an undertaker of industry who unites all these means of production, and who finds in the value of the products which result from them, the re-establishment of the entire capital he employs, and the value of the wages, the interest and the rent which he pays, as well as the profits belonging to himself.

What happens when the value of the products he has created is not sufficient to pay for all that?

He loses, if he has any thing to lose: or if he has nothing, those lose who have given him their confidence.

CHAPTER VIII.
ON THE PROFITS OF INDUSTRY, CAPITAL, AND LAND; THAT IS, INCOME.

What is the source of the profits of industry, capital, and land?

It is in the price of the products created by their co-operation. The consumer in buying a product, pays all the charges of its production, that is, the services of the producers (the industrious, the capitalists, and the landholders), who have contributed to its production.

How can these profits, paid by a single consumer, be distributed among the different producers?

By the advances which the producers make of them to one another.

Explain that by an example.

Let us examine how the value of a cloth coat is distributed among the producers of the stuff of which it is made. We see that a farmer who has reared a sheep, has paid a rent to the landholder who let to him the land on which the sheep was fed. That is a profit received for the productive service of the land. If the farmer has borrowed the capital necessary for the cultivation of his farm, the interest which he pays for it is another profit, received by a capitalist, for the productive service of his capital. When the farmer has sold his wool, the price which he receives for it reimburses to him the rent and interest he has paid, and also the profits of his industry. The clothier, in his turn, by means of his capital, advances this value which is already distributed: if his capital is a borrowed one, and he pays interest for it, he pays also in advance the profits of the capitalist who lent it to him; and he is reimbursed the whole, together with his profits, by the woollen draper, who is at last reimbursed for his advances and his profits by the sale which he makes to the consumer. Thus at the time the sale of the cloth was accomplished, the value had already been distributed among its different producers.

In thus tracing the progress of any product whatever, we shall find that its value is scattered among a crowd of producers, many of whom perhaps are ignorant of the existence of the product: so that a man that wears the coat is perhaps, without suspecting it, one of the capitalists, and consequently one of the producers, who have contributed to its formation.

Is not society then divided into producers and consumers?

Every body consumes, and almost every body produces. For, not to be a producer, it is necessary neither to exercise any industry, nor any talent, nor to possess either the smallest portion of land or of productive capital.

What do the profits, distributed among society, become?

They compose the income of each individual; and the incomes of all the individuals which form a nation, compose the total income of that nation.

What is called annual income?

It is the sum of all the portions of income received in the course of a year. The annual income of a whole nation, is the sum of all the portions of income received, in the course of a year, by all the individuals of which that nation is composed.

Are incomes paid at fixed periods?

Some of them are so; some not. A landholder who lets his land, a capitalist who lends his capital, and who thus gives up to another the profits which may result from these agents of production, generally stipulate the condition of receiving the rent or interest, which forms their income, at fixed periods. The workman who lets out his industrious talent receives the wages which form his income by portions, every week or every fortnight. But the grocer, who sells sugar and coffee, receives on each ounce that he sells, a small portion of his profit, and all these united profits form his income.

Are incomes, or portions of income, always paid in money?

The manner in which they are paid has nothing to do with the subject. The corn, vegetables, milk, and butter, which a farmer consumes in his own family, form part of his income. If he pays part of his rent in provisions, these provisions form part of the income of the landlord. The essential thing is the value paid, whether this value is paid in provisions, or whether he that owes it, exchanges these provisions for money, in order to pay the value in money, is of no importance. It is the value acquired, under what ever form, for a productive service, that constitutes income.

As the incomes of individuals are so much the more considerable as their profits are greater, and as their profits are greater when their productive services are better paid, it appears to me that the dearer these productive services are, the greater the total income of that nation must be.

Yes: but when the productive services are dearer so are the products; and when the price of the products augments in the same proportion as the incomes, the augmentation of the income is only nominal. When the charges of production have doubled, with an income nominally double, we can only purchase the same quantity of products. That alone really increases the ease of individuals and of nations, which lowers the value of products without decreasing incomes.

In what circumstances is this advantage experienced?

It is when, by a better employment of the means of production, the products are multiplied without increasing the charges of production. Then the products fall and incomes remain the same. This is what takes place when a new and ingenious machine has been brought into use, such as the stocking frame and the cotton spinning machines: when a new canal has been cut, which, without increasing the charge, permits the transport of a hundred times more merchandise, &c.

CHAPTER IX.
ON WAGES, INTEREST, AND RENT.

What do you observe on the wages of workmen, interest of capital, and rent of land?

That he who lets out his industry, his capital, or his land, renounces the profits he might have drawn from their productive services; he renounces them in favour of an undertaker of industry, who hires them, and who draws, from these means of production, a profit which is either superior or equal, or inferior, to what he pays for them.

What causes raise the rate of wages?

The abundance of capital and land compared with the number of workmen: for there must be land, and, above all, capital, in order to employ workmen.

Why is it that wages scarcely ever exceed what is necessary to maintain a workman and his family, according to the custom of the place?

Because wages, by rising higher, encourage an increase of workmen; this occasions such services to be more offered in proportion to the demand for them. Works, which require rare and distinguished talents, are exceptions to this rule, because such talents cannot always be increased according to the demand for them.

What causes influence the rate of interest?

The interest of capital lent, although expressed by one price only, a *certain per centage* on the capital lent, ought really to be distinguished into two parts.

Explain that by an example.

If you lend a sum of money, and you agree with the borrower for an interest of six per cent. *per annum,* there is in this rate, four per cent. (more or less), to pay for the productive service of the capital, and two per cent. (more or less) to cover the risk that you run of never getting your capital back.

On what do you found this presumption?

On this, that if you were enabled to lend the same capital with perfect security, on a very safe mortgage, you would lend it at four per cent. more or less. The surplus is then a species of premium of insurance which is paid to you to indemnify you for the risk that you run.

Setting aside the premium of insurance, which varies according to the greater or less solidity of the parties, what are the causes which vary the rate of interest, properly so called?

The rate of interest rises when those who borrow have numerous, ready, and lucrative employments for capital, because then many undertakers of industry are desirous of participating in the profits which these employments of capital offer; and capitalists are also more likely to use them themselves, which augments the demand for capital, and diminishes the amount which is offered for employment. The rate of interest increases also when, from whatever cause, the mass of disposable capital, that is, of capitals requiring to be employed, has been diminished.* Contrary circumstances lower the rate of interest; and one of these circumstances may so balance the other, that the rate of interest will remain at the same point, because the one tends to heighten, precisely as much as the other to lower, the rate.

When you say that the mass of disposable capital increases or diminishes, do you mean by that the quantity of money?

By no means: I mean values destined by their possessors to reproductive consumption, and which are not so engaged that they cannot be withdrawn in order to use them differently.

102

Explain that by an example?

Suppose that you have lent funds to a merchant on condition of his paying them back to you on giving him three months notice; or, which comes to the same thing, that you are in the habit of discounting bills of exchange, can you not easily employ these funds in a different way if you find any one more convenient to you?

Without doubt.

Then these funds are a disposable capital. They are so too, if they are in the form of a merchandise easily sold, since you can exchange them readily for any other value. They are still more disposable if they are in specie; but you must understand that the sum of all these disposable capitals is a very different thing from the sum of coined money, and that it may be much more considerable.

I understand so.

Well! it is the sum of these capitals which influences the rate of interest, and not the sums of money under which form these values temporarily present themselves when they are about to pass from one hand to another. A disposable capital may be in the form of a certain sort of merchandise, a sack of guineas for instance: but if the quantity of this merchandise which is in circulation, has no influence on the rate of interest, the abundance or the scarcity of the gold has no influence on it either.

It is not then really the hire of money that one pays when one pays an interest?

By no means.

Why is it called the interest of money?

From very inaccurate ideas which are formed of the nature and use of capital.

What is legal interest?

It is the rate fixed by the law in cases where it has not been fixed by the parties: as when the holder of a capital has enjoyed it in the place of an absentee, or a minor to whom he is bound to account.

Cannot public authority fix a limit to the interest which individuals may agree upon?

It cannot, without violating the freedom of transactions.

What causes influence the rent of land?

The demand for the hire of farms compared with the number to be let. It may be observed on this subject, that the demand commonly exceeds the number to be let, because in all countries the number of these is necessarily limited; while that of farmers and of capitals, which may be applied to this industry, are not necessarily so: so that in those places, where there are not stronger motives to a contrary effect, rent is rather above than below the real profit of land.

What have you more to say on this subject?

That rent tends nevertheless to get down to the profit of land; for when it exceeds it, the farmer is obliged to pay the excess, either out of the profits of his industry, or the interest of his capital; and is no longer completely indemnified for the employment of those means of production.

Notes

[*] See some striking examples in my *Treatise on Political Economy,* liv. ii. chap. 8.

CHAPTER X.
ON INCOMES FOUNDED ON IMMATERIAL PRODUCTS.

What is meant by immaterial products?

They express a utility produced, but which is not attached to any material.

Explain that by an example.

When a physician visits a sick person and prescribes a remedy or a regimen which cures him, he renders himself useful to him. The physician receives a sum of money in exchange for this utility: but here the utility is not attached to any merchandise where it may be preserved for a time, and exchanged again. It is a product truly immaterial, in exchange for which the physician receives a fee which constitutes his income. The industry of the physician is analogous to that of every undertaker of an industry. He applies to the wants of men the medical knowledge which he has collected.

What other professions found their incomes on immaterial products?

There are a great number of them. They include the most elevated as well as the most abject situations in society. The public functionaries, from the chiefs of the government down to the lowest officer, the judges and the priests, receive in exchange for their usefulness to the public, fees paid at the expense of the public.

What causes influence the amount of these fees?

As these fees are never the result of a free agreement, but depend on political circumstances, they are seldom proportioned with exactness to the utility produced.

Give me some other examples of industry productive of immaterial products.

An advocate, an actor, a musician, a soldier, a domestic, render services of which the value may be measured by the price which they receive.

What do you observe respecting immaterial products?

That they are necessarily consumed at the same instant they are produced. Their value, consequently, cannot be reserved for consumption at any other time, or to be employed as capital, because they are not attached to any material by means of which they can be preserved.

What consequence do you draw from that?

That in multiplying the services rendered by these different classes, the consumption of them is multiplied: that it hinders these kind of works from contributing to the increase of the mass of wealth. It follows from this, that in multiplying, for example, placemen, lawyers, soldiers, &c. the wealth of a country is not increased, whatever may otherwise be the utility of these different professions. The services they render exist no longer than the moment they are performed.

They live then on the incomes of other producers?

They live no more on the incomes of other producers than a wine merchant lives on the income of a woollen draper, who buys wine which he pays for with part of his income, and afterwards consumes. An actor is a dealer in amusement; a spectator buys his commodity, pays for it out of his income, and consumes it the instant it is delivered to him. The products furnished by the actor and by the wine merchant, are equally lost; but when the price which has been given to them for it has been freely paid, it is an exchange like all others, followed by a consumption of the same nature as all improductive consumptions.

Are immaterial products the fruit of industry alone?

Yes, when nothing has been advanced to acquire the talent of which they are the fruit: but when this talent has required long and expensive studies they are the result of an *appropriated capital**, that is to say, of advances which have been made of industry. One part of the fees then serves to pay the life interest in this capital, and another to pay for the industry exercised. When the fees, or gratuities, are not sufficient to pay for the service of these two agents of production, their product becomes more scarce, and its price increases until the moment when the quantity of that product is rendered equal to the demand.

Are there any immaterial products which are the result of capital alone?

Yes, if moveable effects (household furniture) are considered as capital, and if they are kept up to their original value. When their value is not kept up, besides the use of the capital, a part of the capital itself is consumed.

The plate which is used in a family forms part of the capital and riches of that family. It is not improductive since it renders a daily service, but it does not produce any value which can afterwards be exchanged for any other thing. This service is an immaterial product consumed at the moment. The family consumes the interest of this part of its capital.

Are there any immaterial products which result from land?

Yes: the enjoyment received from a pleasure garden, is a product of the land of this garden and the capital devoted to its arrangement. It has no other exchangeable product.

Notes

[*] It must be remembered that an *appropriated capital* is a capital which cannot be withdrawn from the employment to which it has been applied, to be applied to another employment.

CHAPTER XI.
ON CONSUMPTION IN GENERAL.

We have already seen what consumption is: finish the development of its effects.

It must be remembered that to consume is not to destroy the matter of a product: we can no more destroy the matter than we can create it. To consume is to destroy its value by destroying its utility; by destroying the quality which had been given to it, of being useful to, or of satisfying the wants of man. Then the quality for which it had been demanded was destroyed. The demand having ceased, the value, which exists always in proportion to the demand, ceases also. The thing thus consumed, that is, whose value is destroyed, though the material is not, no longer forms any portion of wealth.

A product may be consumed rapidly, as food, or slowly, as a house; it may be consumed in part, as a coat, which, having been worn for some months, still retains a certain value. In whatever manner the consumption takes place, the effect is the same: it is a destruction of value; and as value makes riches, consumption is a destruction of wealth.

What is the object of consumption?

To procure to the consumer either an enjoyment or a new value, in general superior to the value consumed, otherwise the consumer would not obtain any profit. In the first case it is an *improductive,* and in the second a *reproductive* consumption.

What would that consumption be which had for its object neither to procure an enjoyment, nor to create a new product?

That would be a sacrifice without compensation; a folly.

What must be thought then of a system, the tendency of which is, to consume for the sole purpose of favouring production?

That which must be thought of a system which should propose to burn down a city, for the purpose of benefiting the builders, by employing them to restore it.

Develope what relates to reproductive consumption.

Every thing which has been said on production, serves for that purpose.

What have you to say on the subject of improductive consumption?

Improductive consumption, which we shall hereafter, for shortness, call simply *consumption,* divides itself into two kinds, *private* and *public.*

What do you understand by private consumption?

That which has for its object to satisfy the wants of individual and of families.

What do you mean by public consumption?

That which has for its object to supply the wants of men whose association forms a community, a province, or a nation.

Are these two sorts of consumption of the same nature?

They are entirely of the same nature, and their effects are the same. One set of persons cause the consumption in one case, and other persons in the other; that is all the difference.

What is meant by these words, annual consumption of a nation?

It is the sum of the values consumed by a nation in a year, whether for the wants of individuals or of the public.

Do these words comprehend reproductive consumption as well as the others?

Yes; for we may say that France consumes annually so many quintals of soda or of indigo, although the indigo and the soda can only be consumed reproductively, as they cannot satisfy directly any want; and as they can be employed only in the arts, they serve necessarily for reproduction.

Do you comprehend in the consumption of a nation, the merchandize she exports to other countries?

Yes; and I comprehend in its products whatever it receives in return; in the same manner that I comprehend in its consumption the value of the wool it uses for the manufacture of cloth, and in its productions the value of the cloth which results from it.

Does a nation consume all that it produces?

Yes, with very few exceptions; for it is our interest not to create products unless they are demanded, and they are never demanded but to be consumed.

If a nation consumes the total of the values which it produces, how can it accumulate values, form capital, and maintain it?

The values, which serve the purposes of capital, may be consumed perpetually, yet are never lost, for in the same proportion as they are consumed they are reproduced under new forms by the action of industry. This reproduction, once accomplished, if the value reproduced is found superior to the value consumed, there has been an augmentation of capital. In the contrary case, a diminution of capital. If the reproduction has simply equalled the consumption, the capital has been merely kept up.*

Shew me the application of these truths by examples.

Take, for instance, a farmer, or a manufacturer, or even a merchant. Suppose that he employs in his enterprize a capital of twenty thousand pounds, that is to say, suppose that all the values that he has in his enterprize on the first day of a year, are equal in value to a sum of twenty thousand pounds. In the course of his operations these values change their forms perpetually; and although his capital does not exceed twenty thousand pounds, yet we may suppose, that if all the values which he has consumed in the course of the year were added together, they would amount to sixty thousand pounds, because a value destroyed may have been reproduced, destroyed again a second and a third time before the year revolves. We may suppose also, that if all the values produced in the same year were added together they might amount to a sum of sixty-four thousand pounds. If then this undertaker of industry has had consumption for sixty thousand pounds, and productions for sixty-four thousand pounds, he ought to have at the end of the year values amounting to four thousand pounds more than he had at the beginning.

That appears clear to me.

Let us go on. If he has expended improductively in the same year, to satisfy the wants of his family four thousand pounds, he will have consumed his profits; and if he takes his inventory he will find himself, at the end of the year, with a-capital of twenty thousand pounds only, as he had at the beginning of the year. But if, instead of having expended improductively for the support of his family four thousand pounds, he had only expended two thousand, unless he has hid two thousand pounds, he will find that this value of two thousand pounds, which has not been expended improductively, will have been laid out productively, and that it will appear in his inventory in augmentation of capital under some form or other, either under that of provisions, of goods in process of manufacture, or even of advances capable of being recovered.

I conceive that.

You perceive then, that although the value of the capital has not been more than twenty thousand pounds, the total value of the products for the year may have been much more considerable?

Yes.

That this form of products, whatever it may be, may have been entirely consumed, and that, nevertheless, the capital of this individual may have been augmented.

Yes.

Well, then, multiply in your mind what has happened to a single individual, and suppose that the same thing has happened to all the individuals of the same nation: or at least suppose that the consequences that have happened to some, balanced by those which have happened to others, have produced a general result analogous to the preceding example, and you will find, by a second example, that a nation which had at the commencement of the year a capital of a hundred millions, may have consumed in a year three hundred millions of values, producing three hundred and twenty millions of values, of which she has consumed reproductively three hundred millions, and improductively twenty millions; or rather reproductively three hundred and ten millions, and improductively ten millions.

I grant it.

In this last supposition this little nation, which will have consumed all its productions, will, nevertheless, be enriched during the year ten millions of values, which will be found distributed under different forms among those individuals who have conducted their affairs with the greatest intelligence and economy.

Notes

[*] In the amount of reproductive consumptions the profits of all the industries employed, even that of the undertaker must always be included. When all the charges of production, (the profits included), are paid, and the capital is not completely reestablished in its full value, the consumption exceeds the reproduction: there is a loss.

CHAPTER XII.
ON PRIVATE CONSUMPTION.

What difference is there between the words Expence *and* Consumption?

Expence is the purchase of a thing to be consumed, and as, in general, one only buys what one intends to consume, the words *expence* and *consumption* are often used for one another. It is, however, proper to remark, that when one buys a product, we exchange the value we are willing to give up for one of which we are in want: the value of a crown, for instance, for the value of a handkerchief. We are still as rich when we have made the purchase as we were before, only we possess in the form of a handkerchief what we before had in the form of a crown. We do not begin to lose this value until we begin to use the handkerchief, and it is only when the consumption is finished that we are poorer by a crown. It is not then in buying, but in consuming, that we dissipate our property. That is the reason why, in the middle ranks of life, the character and economical talents of the woman, who directs the greater part of the consumption of the family, assists materially to preserve fortunes.

What do you understand by economical talents?

It is the talent of deciding judiciously what consumption may be permitted, and what must be prohibited, in that state of fortune in which we are placed, and according to the income we have.

What do you understand by avarice?

We are avaricious when we deprive ourselves, or those dependent upon us, of those consumptions which we might permit according to our incomes.

Is it avaricious not to expend the whole of one's income?

No; for it is only by the savings which are made from improductive consumption, that we can hope to enjoy repose in our old days, and to procure an establishment for our families.

Do we do any wrong to society by thus amassing a productive capital, for the sake of enjoying ourselves, or suffering those belonging to us to enjoy, the profits it will produce?

On the contrary, capitals, accumulated by individuals, add so much to the total capital of society; and as a capital placed, that is, employed reproductively, is indispensably necessary to give activity to industry, every person who spares from his revenue to add to his capital, procures, to a certain number of persons who have nothing but their industry, the means of deriving a revenue from their talents.

Are not some consumptions better managed than others?

Yes: they are those which procure greater satisfaction, in proportion to the sacrifice of the values which they occasion. Such are the consumptions which satisfy the real, rather than fictitious, wants. Wholesome food, decent clothing, convenient lodgings, are consumptions more fitting and better regulated than luxurious food, foppish clothing, and stately habitations. More true satisfaction results from the first than the last.

What do you consider besides as well regulated consumptions?

The consumption of products of the best quality of every sort, although they may cost more.

For what reason do you consider them as well regulated consumptions?

Because the workmanship employed on a bad article will be more quickly consumed than that on a good one. When a pair of shoes is made with bad leather, the work of the shoemaker, which is used up in the same time as the shoes, does not cost less, and is consumed in fifteen days instead of lasting two or three months, which it would have done if the leather had been good. The carriage of bad merchandize costs as much as that of good, which is more advantageous. Poor nations have, consequently, beside the disadvantage of consuming less perfect productions, that of paying dearer for them in proportion.

What consumptions do you consider as the worst regulated?

Those which procure more chagrin and mischief than satisfaction: such as the excess of intemperance, and expences which excite contempt, or are followed by punishment.

CHAPTER XIII.
ON PUBLIC CONSUMPTION.

What do you call public consumptions?

Those which are made for the service of men, assembled in communities, provinces, or nations. It is the purchase of services and products, consumed for public utility, which constitute the public expences.

What are the principal objects of public expences?

The payment of the administrators of the government, the judges, soldiers, and professors in the public institutions; the providing for the army and navy, and maintaining the public establishments, edifices, roads, canals, ports, hospitals, &c.

What do you observe generally with respect to public expences?

That the public is never so cheaply served as individuals.

What are the reasons?

There are three. First, that political circumstances fix the number and salaries of the public functionaries, and that their services are consequently not open to a free competition. The second, that those who direct the public expences, devoting to them money which is not their own, are less sparing of it than individuals would be. The third, that works executed for the public, are less easily superintended, and are never watched by personal interest.

I am inclined to believe that public consumptions, by returning to society the money which has been drawn from it, do not impoverish it.

They do impoverish it the same as private consumptions, by the whole amount of the values consumed.

How do you explain this?

The money is wrested from the people without equivalent. A value is taken away from the community, without its receiving any other value in return. But when this money is returned to the community, it is not gratuitously; it is in virtue of a purchase in which the seller delivers to government, or its agents, things which have a value. The community has twice delivered the same value. It has delivered the contribution, and also the merchandize, which the government has bought with the amount of that contribution. Of these two values the one is returned by the purchase which the government has made; the other is never returned at all: it is consumed, that is to say, it is destroyed.

Illustrate this by an example.

We will suppose that a community pays in money a hundred thousand pounds; there is a value equal to one hundred thousand pounds drawn from the community. The agents of the government, with this sum, purchase clothes for the army; this is another value equal to one hundred thousand pounds drawn from the community. The government, in paying the clothier, restores the one hundred thousand pounds it had raised by contribution: but the value of the one hundred thousand pounds in clothes is not restored, and will be consumed and lost. It is the same case with that of a man who draws from the community his revenue in money, and returns it back by means of his expenditure; but who does not return the provisions he has purchased with his revenue, and which he has consumed.

But when a government constructs buildings, and with the amount of the contributions pays the workmen, does it not then restore to society the values which it has drawn from it?

Not an atom more. It draws from society, in this last case, one value in contribution, and then another value equal to it in services which it consumes. The purchase of the services is not a restitution, but an exchange.

Is not this a mere distinction of words, and is not the purchase of services equivalent to a restitution?

Not in the least. When the government employs workmen, it receives from them in exchange for their wages a real value, which is their labour; a value founded on the products which are to result from this labour; a value, which being consumed by the government, cannot be consumed in any other design, nor with any other result.

The workmen thus employed would have perhaps been without work?

Why? The government by this operation has not multiplied the values appropriated to the payment of workmen. If it distributes them on the one hand, it takes away from the contributor on the other, the power of distributing them, either directly, by employing the workmen himself, or indirectly, by means of his consumptions.

When a government consumes, it stands then in the same situation with any other consumer?

Almost always; the exceptions to this rule are too rare to be worth noticing.

What consequences do you draw from it?

That the consumptions, or, if you will, the expences of government, are always a sacrifice made by society, which is never indemnified for it, otherwise than by the product which results from it.

What do you mean by a product resulting from public expenditure?

When the government constructs a bridge, the service which the public derive from it, repays, and often with very great advantage, the sacrifice of values which the bridge has cost. But no benefit results from the mere expenditure of the money, nor the employment of the workmen employed on its construction; for, if this money had remained in the hands of the contributors, it would either directly or indirectly have put in activity an equal quantity of industry.

When a part of the contributions is employed in the construction of monuments or buildings, which have no public utility, there is then on the part of society a sacrifice without compensation?

Precisely: it is for that reason that a good government makes no expenditure which has not a useful result. The economy of nations is exactly the same with that of individuals.

CHAPTER XIV.
ON PUBLIC PROPERTY AND TAXES.

From whence are the values derived which serve for the public consumptions?

They are derived either from the revenues of property belonging to the public, or from taxes.

What constitutes the revenues of public property?

These properties are either, capital or freehold property, but most generally freehold property, land, houses, &c. which the government let, and the revenue of which it consumes for the advantage of the public. When it consists of forests, it sells the annual felling; when capital it lends it at interest, but this last case is very rare.

Who is it that pays the taxes?

The individuals who in this respect we call *contributors.*

Where do the contributors get the values with which they pay the taxes?

They take these values from the products which belong to them, or which comes to the same thing, from the money which they procure by the exchange of these products.

Are these products the fruit of the annual productions?

They are sometimes the products of the year, which form part of the income of individuals, and sometimes former products, which they employ as productive capitals.

In what case do the contributors take from their capitals to pay the taxes?

When their incomes are not sufficient. And in this case the taxes dry up one of the sources of revenue, and one of the means of the industry of society.

Give me an example in which the taxes are discharged with a portion of capital.

If a man whose income is absorbed by the ordinary contributions, together with the maintenance of his family, comes to an heritance, and as an heir he is bound to pay impost, it must be taken out of his inheritance; the capital in the hands of the heir is therefore no longer so considerable as it was in the hands of the deceased. Similar observations may be made on the expenses of proceedings at law, bonds, securities, &c. In all these cases the tax paid by the contributor is withdrawn from the mass of capital usefully employed, and is so much capital devoted to consumption, and actually disappears. This happens also in cases where the profits are small and the impost considerable; many contributors cannot in that case discharge the taxes without breaking in upon their capitals.

The major part of the taxes are however taken from incomes?

Yes: for if the taxes dry up too completely the sources of production, they would diminish more and more every day the products with which alone they could be paid.

If there are some of them which break into the capital of individuals, how happens it that the means of production are not destroyed in the long run?

Because at the same time that some individuals break into their capitals, those of others are increased by saving.

Do not the taxes serve, on the other hand, to multiply products by compelling the contributors to produce, in order to be able to pay them?

The hope of enjoying the products one has created is a much stronger incitement to production than the idea of satisfying the tax gatherer. But if the impost should excite the desire of producing more it does not afford the means. In order to extend production it is necessary to increase capital, which is the more impossible, as the necessity of paying the tax prevents the saving, which alone creates capital. In short, if the necessity of paying the taxes should excite efforts which augment production, there will not result from it any increase of the general riches, since what is raised by the impost is consumed, and does not serve to increase any saving. Thus it may be seen that great taxes are destructive of public prosperity instead of being favourable to it.

Which are the principal kinds of taxes levied for this purpose?

Sometimes they are exacted from the contributors at so much per head, as in the capitation tax. Sometimes as in the land tax, they take a part of the revenue arising from the lands; which are valued, either after the actual rent or after the extent and fertility of the soil. Sometimes the rent of a house, the number of its doors and windows, and of the servants and horses kept by the contributor, serve as a basis for the amount of his contribution. Sometimes, his profits are valued according to the industry he carries on: from hence the impost on licences *(patentes)*. All these contributions bear the name of *direct taxes,* because they are demanded, *directly,* of the contributor in person.

Are not all taxes demanded directly from the contributor?

They are sometimes demanded, not from the payer, but are included in the price of the merchandize on which the impost is laid, and without the receiver knowing even the name of the contributor. For this reason they are called *indirect taxes.*

When and in what manner are taxes levied on merchandize?

They are sometimes levied at the instant in which they are produced, like the salt in France, or the gold and silver mines in Mexico. A portion of the value of these merchandize is levied at the moment of their extraction. Sometimes a duty is levied at the moment of their transportation from one place to another, as in the instance of import duties; and in the "Octroi," which is paid in France at the entrance of towns: sometimes at the moment of consumption, as for stamps and admissions to the theatres.

Does the amount of the impost remain at the expense of those who pay it?

No: they endeavour to reimburse themselves at least in part from those who purchase the products in the creation of which the contributors have assisted.

Do the contributors always succeed in thus shifting the burden from themselves?

They seldom succeed completely, because they cannot do so without raising the price of their products; and a rise of price always diminishes the consumption of a product by putting it out of the reach of some of its consumers. The demand for this sort of product then diminishes, and its price falls. The price not then affording so liberal a remuneration for the productive services devoted to this object, the quantity of it is lessened. Thus when an import duty is laid on cotton, the manufacturers of cottons and the tradesmen who sell them cannot raise the price so high as to recover back the amount of the taxes; for that purpose it would be necessary that the same quantity of cotton goods should be demanded and sold, and that the society should devote to the purchase of this particular article more values than it had heretofore devoted to it, which is not possible. The cotton goods become dearer; their producers gain less, and this kind of production declines.

What consequence do you draw from that?

That the impost is paid partly by the producers, whose profits, i. e. whose incomes it lessens; and partly by those consumers who continue to purchase notwithstanding the dearness, since they pay more for a product, which in point of fact is not more valuable.

What other consequence do you draw faom it?

That the impost, in making the products dearer, does not augment even nominally the total value of productions; for the products diminish in quantity more than they augment in price.

Does this effect take place with respect to any other merchandize than that on which the impost is levied?

It takes place on all the merchandise which the contributor sells. Brewers and bakers sell their products dearer when a tax is laid on the wood or coals which they burn. A tax on meat and other eatables at the gates of a city renders all its manufactured products dearer.

Can all producers make the consumers bear a portion of the imposts which they are compelled to pay?

There are producers who cannot. An impost laid on an article of luxury bears only on those who consume it. If a tax is laid on lace, the wine merchant whose wife wears lace, cannot sell his wine dearer on that account, for he could not maintain a competition with his neighbour whose wife does not wear lace. A landholder cannot in general make his consumers bear any portion of the tax he is compelled to pay.*

In order not to deceive ourselves as to the effect of taxes, how ought we to consider them?

As a cause of the destruction of part of the products of society. This destruction takes place at the expense of those who are unable to evade or shift it from themselves. The producers and consumers pay the value of the products thus destroyed; the first, in not selling their products at a price sufficient to cover the taxes; the second, in paying more for them than they are worth, but in proportions which vary with every article and every class of individuals.

We may also consider the impost as an augmentation of the charges of production. It is an expense sustained by the producers and consumers; but which while it renders the products dearer, does not augment the incomes of the producers, as its amount is not divided among them. Their expenses augment as consumers without their incomes increasing as producers: they are not so rich.

What is to be understood by a subject of taxation?

By those words, is often meant, the merchandise which serves as a basis for the tax. Brandy, in this sense, is a "subject of taxation," by means of the duties which are levied on this liquor. But the expression is not correct. Brandy is only a basis for the demand of a value; a merchandise which the government uses as a means of raising money. The true subject of taxation is, in this case, the income of the individuals who manufacture and consume the brandy. Thus the subject of taxation increases, when these incomes, whatever be their source, are augmented.

What do you conclude from that?

That every thing which tends to increase the riches of a nation extends and multiplies the subject of taxation. It is from this cause, that as a country prospers the amount of the taxes increases, without increasing the rate of them; and diminishes when it declines.

Are we justified in considering the amount of the taxes as part of the income of a nation?

Never, for they are values not created but transferred. They have formed a part of the incomes of individuals which they have not consumed.

Have not the government other sources of revenue?

Sometimes the government retains the exclusive exercise of a certain industry, and causes it to be paid for beyond its value, as the carriage of letters. In this case the tax does not amount to the whole of the charge for postage, but only to that part which exceeds what it would cost if this service was left open to free competition.

The profits which government sometimes makes on lotteries is of the same kind, but is much less justifiable on many accounts.

Notes

[*] So long as the tax does not absorb the whole of the net profit, or rent of land, it is worth while to cultivate it: consequently the impost does not diminish the quantity of the territorial products which come to market, and this is never a cause of dearness. When the impost is excessive, it surpasses the net produce of the worst lands, and hinders the improvement of others. Thus territorial products become more rare: still this circumstance does not raise the price in a durable manner, because the population is not long before it gets down to the level of the territorial products; if less are offered less are wanted. For this reason, in these countries which produce little corn, it is not dearer than in those that produce much. It is even cheaper, for reasons which cannot be developed here.

CHAPTER XV.
ON PUBLIC LOANS.

With what view do governments borrow money?

To provide for extraordinary expences which the ordinary revenues are not sufficient to discharge.

How do they pay the interest of the loans they borrow?

They pay it either by laying on a new tax, or by economising, from the ordinary expences, a sum sufficient to pay the annual interest.

Loans, then, are a means of consuming a principal of which the interest is paid by a portion of the taxes?

Yes.

Who are the lenders?

Individuals who have capitals at their disposal.

Since government represents the society, and society is composed of individuals, it is then the society which lends to itself?

Yes: it is a part of the individuals who lend to the whole of the individuals; that is to say, to the society or to its government.

What effect is produced by public loans on the public riches? Do they augment or diminish them?

The loan in itself neither increases nor diminishes them: it is a value which passes from the hands of individuals to the hands of the government, a simple transfer. But as the principal of the loan, or, if you will, the capital lent, is generally consumed in consequence of this transfer, public loans produce an improductive consumption, a destruction of capital.

Would not a capital thus lent have been equally consumed if it had remained in the hands of individuals?

No: the individuals who lent the capital, wished to lay it out, not to consume it. If it had not been lent to government it would have been lent to those who would have made use of it, or they would have employed it themselves; thus the capital would have been consumed reproductively instead of improductively.

Is the total income of a nation increased or diminished by public loans?

It is diminished, because all the capital which is consumed carries with it the income which it would otherwise have gained.

But in this case, the individual who lends does not lose any income, since the government pays him interest for his capital; and if he does not lose, who does?

Those who lose are the contributors who pay the increased taxes, with which the public creditor is paid his interest.

But if the creditor receives on the one hand an income which the contributor pays on the other, it appears to me that there is no portion of income lost, and that the state has profited by the principal of the loan which it has consumed.

You are in an error; and to convince you of it we will examine how this operation is effected. An individual lends to the state a thousand pounds. Consequently he draws this value from an employment in which it was already, or in which it would have been engaged. Supposing that this employment would have afforded five per cent. there is an income of fifty pounds taken from the society. It is nevertheless paid to the creditor; but how is it paid? At the expence of a contributor; of a landed proprietor, who would have used for his own purposes these fifty pounds which the government takes from him to pay the creditor. Instead of two incomes which there was in society, that of the thousand pounds lent to government (which either had been, or might have been placed elsewhere) and the income of the funds, which had produced to the landholder the fifty pounds of contribution, which he has been compelled to pay to satisfy the creditor. In lieu of these two incomes, there remains but one, namely, the last, which is transferred from the contributor to the creditor. Why is there only one income of fifty pounds where there had been formerly two? Because there had been, beside the funds of the contributor, another fund of one thousand pounds, producing fifty pounds, which has been lent and consumed, and which, consequently, produces nothing.*

What are the principal forms under which a government pays the interest of its loans?

Sometimes it pays a perpetual interest on the capital lent, which it does not bind itself to repay: the lenders have in this case no other means of recovering their capital than to sell their debt to other individuals who desire to place themselves in the situation of the former.

Sometimes it borrows, by way of annuity, and pays the lender a life interest.

Sometimes it borrows on condition of repayment, and it stipulates a pure and simple repayment, in a certain number of years, by instalments; or a reimbursement of the principal sum at periods which are sometimes determined by lot.

Sometimes it negociates bills on its agents, the receivers of contributions. The loss which it suffers by discount represents the interest on the advances it receives.

Sometimes it sells public offices, and thus pays interest for the money furnished. The incumbent can never get back his principal without selling his office. The price of offices is often paid under the name of security.

All these modes of borrowing have the effect of withdrawing from productive employment capitals which are consumed in the public service.

Have not the government the means of paying their debts, even those of which it has promised to pay the interest perpetually?

Yes; by means of what is called a *sinking fund.*

What is a sinking fund?

When a tax is laid upon the people to pay the interest of a loan, it is laid a little heavier than is necessary to pay this interest; this excess is confided to what are called commissioners for the management of the *sinking fund,* and who employ it every year to buy up at the market price a part of the interest or annuities paid by the state. As the same interest always continues to be paid, the sinking fund devotes in the year following, to the purchase of these interests, not only the portion of the tax which is devoted to this use in the first instance, but also the interest which it has already bought up. This manner of extinguishing the public debt by its progressively increasing action, would extinguish it with sufficient rapidity if these sinking funds were never diverted from this object, and if the debts were not kept up by a perpetual addition of new loans, which bring annually into the market more interest than the sinking fund buys up.

Notes

[*] See in my *Treatise of Political Economy,* 2d edit. book. iii. c. 9. a synoptical table of the progress of these values.

CHAPTER XVI.
ON PROPERTY, AND THE NATURE OF RICHES.

Can riches exist where there is no property?

No: for riches being composed of the value of the things which we possess, there can be no riches where no things are possessed; that is, no property.

Into how many classes can things possessed be arranged?

Into two grand classes: that which constitutes stock, and that which constitutes income.

What do you observe relative to the riches which constitute income?

That having been created without affecting our stock, they may be consumed without encroaching upon it; and that if we do not consume them improductively, they will increase our stock.

Do you not sub-divide that which constitutes our stock?

Yes: our stock may consist,

1st. Of land and other natural agents of which we are acknowledged proprietors;

2d. Of capital, or values produced, which we devote to reproduction:

3d. Of faculties, or talents, natural and acquired, which we employ for the same purpose.

What do you observe relatively to the riches which constitute our stock?

That we can alienate the property of the first two kinds of stock (our lands and our capitals) but not that of the third kind (our industrious talents). That we can let out to use all the three kinds. That the last is a life property, which perishes with us.

What have you further to observe respecting them?

That not being applicable to the satisfying of our wants, or of procuring enjoyments, because they are appropiated to reproduction, they are of no value, except for the faculty which they have of contributing to the production of some other consumable values. The demand which there exists for consumable values, that is, for products, establishes a demand for the stock which is capable of producing, that is, for land, capital, and industrious talents; this demand establishes their value, and this value makes a part of the riches of those to whom they belong.

Why have not a great number of natural agents necessary to production, as the heat of the sun, the air of the atmosphere; why have not these a value?

Because there is no demand for their productive faculties; and there is no demand for them, because when these faculties are present they exceed all wants, and are accessible to all mankind: and when they are not present, no person can provide them, because no one can appropriate them.

What results from this fact in relation to the value of products?

That when nature lends, gratuitously, her powers to the creation of products, the charges are less than when we must pay for assistance, and that we obtain consequently, products at a cheaper rate. It is for that reason that the grapes of the south do not cost so much as those of the north, which are raised in hot-houses.

You have said that riches are proportioned to the value of the things we possess, that is, that they are so much the greater as the values we possess are greater; have you any thing to add to this subject?

Riches are proportioned to the values we possess, or rather are only those values themselves: but these values are great or small in comparison with the price of the things which may be obtained for them. In other words, if with a certain sum in land, in capital, and in income, I can obtain the things I am in want of at half the price I have hitherto obtained them, by that alone, my riches are doubled.

Thus a nation which does not possess in nominal value more than one half what another nation possesses, will nevertheless be as rich, if she can procure all the products of which she is in want at half the price the other nation is obliged to pay.

The very height of riches, however few values one might possess, would be to be able to procure for nothing all the objects we wished to consume.

We should be at the lowest ebb of poverty, however immense might be the values we possessed, if the value of the things we wanted to consume exceeded the price which we were able to pay for them.

In what does the dearness and cheapness of things consist?

We will examine that in the next chapter.

CHAPTER XVII.
ON THE REAL AND NOMINAL PRICE.

Give me some just ideas on the price of things?

If you wish to form just ideas on this subject you must never confound the *nominal price* with the *real price* of things.

What do you call the nominal price *of things?*

The price we pay for a thing in money or in coin.

What do you call its real price?

The value we have given to obtain the money with which we purchase this thing.

Give me an example.

A potter is in want of a loaf of bread, which sells for a shilling: he is obliged, in order to obtain it, to sell a vase which is worth a shilling. If the price of the loaf should rise to two shillings; and if the potter is obliged to sell two vases in order to obtain these two shillings, which he must pay for the loaf, the dearness of the bread is *real*. If the potter can obtain these two shillings by the sale of a single vase, the dearness of the bread is only *nominal*. He has in both cases exchanged only one vase against one loaf, whatever may have been the denomination of the intermediate value. It is the value of the money which is depreciated, that of the bread has remained the same.

Is it not a real *dearness to a man whose income arises from lands which are let, or from a capital lent at interest, when the loaf has risen from one to two shillings?*

No: that which is real is the depreciation which has taken place in the value of the merchandise in which his income is stipulated to be paid: that is, in the fall of the money. He who pays the income, by acquiring at less expense this merchandise, gains in this case what the other loses.

You have said that if, when I am obliged to give two shillings to buy a loaf, I am able to obtain these two shillings, on the same terms that I before obtained one, the loaf has not become dearer; but if to obtain two shillings, that is, the price of one loaf, I am obliged to give two vases instead of one, then the bread will have really become dearer?

No; not if the vases as well as the money have fallen to half their value.

How can I tell whether they have fallen to half their value or not?

They have fallen if they can be obtained for half the expenses of production: that is, if means have been found to create, at the same charge of production (which consists as we know of the workmanship, interest of capital and profit) two vases instead of one.

It is then the lowering the charges of production which causes the real fall in the price of products?

Just so. Then whatever may be the value with which a product is purchased, this product, which has fallen one half, is obtained for one half less expense of production.

Explain that by an example.

If, by means of a knitting frame, I can make a pair of stockings for three shillings, instead of expending six shillings on them, he who grows wheat can obtain a pair of stockings for one half the quantity of wheat which he had before been accustomed to give for them. That is, if he was before obliged to sell thirty-six pounds of wheat in order to obtain a pair of stockings, he would now sell but eighteen. But the eighteen pounds have required on his part only one half the expenses of production which the thirty-six pounds would have required.

It is the same whatever is the production with which we are occupied. It may be said, that when an article really falls in price, not only those who produce it, but every body else, obtains it at the price of the reduced charge of production.

You have said besides that the riches of society is composed of the sum total of the values which it possesses: it appears to me to follow, that the fall of a product, stockings for example, by diminishing the sum of the values belonging to society, diminishes the mass of its riches.

The sum of the riches of society does not fall on that account. Two pairs of stockings are produced instead of one; and two pairs at three shillings are worth as much as one pair at six shillings. The income of society remains the same, for the maker gains as much on two pairs at three shillings, as he did on one pair at six shillings.

But, when the income remains the same, and the products fall, the society is really enriched. If the same fall takes place on all products at once, which is not absolutely impossible, society by obtaining all the objects of its consumption at half price, without having lost any part of its income, would really be twice as rich as before, and could buy twice as many things.

This does not generally happen, but it has happened to a great number of products, which have fallen from the price they were formerly at, some a tenth, some a fourth, a half, three-fourths, as silver, and even in a greater proportion as silks, and probably many other articles.

To what cause is that to be attributed?

To many causes: but principally to the progress of intelligence and industry. It is to their progress that we owe, both the discovery of countries in which there is a greater abundance of products, and also a means of transporting them less hazardous and more economical.

To that progress also we are indebted for processes more simple and more expeditious, the use of machinery, and in general a better adaptation of the productive faculties of nature.

Are there any products which have really become dearer?

There are some, but very few, and only those the demand for which has increased in consequence of the progress of civilization, without the means of production having increased in the same proportion. Such as butchers' meat and poultry, and almost all the useful animals which are raised at less expense in less civilized countries.

Are there not variations in value which are not the consequence of the charges of production?

The errors, the fears or the passions of men, or unforeseen events, cause disorder and confusion in values which are merely relative: that is, when any merchandise rises or falls with respect to others, in consequence of circumstances foreign to its production. Late frosts increase the price of the last years wines, whatever may have been the charges of their production.

Does such a dearness increase the national wealth?

No: for in exchanging another product for one which has become dearer, one must give *more* to receive *less*: he who buys, loses on his merchandise, precisely as much as the seller gains on his goods.

When the wine doubles its price, he, who, to purchase a piece of wine is obliged to sell six bushels of wheat instead of three, which should have purchased a piece of wine is poorer by all that the wine merchant is richer.

Thus these kinds of variation, which sometimes overturn private fortunes, do not affect the general riches* .

Notes

[*] The changes in values which take from a man that property which he did not deserve to lose to give it to another who did not deserve to gain it, are nevertheless mischievous to the general prosperity. They inflict more evil on him who loses than they confer benefit on him who gains: they disappoint the wisest calculations; they discourage the most useful speculations, they divert capitals which were in full productive activity, &c. &c.

CHAPTER XVIII.
ON MONEY.

If money is nothing but merchandise, why is coined silver of greater value than the same weight of silver uncoined?

For the same reasons that a silver tea-pot is worth more than the same weight of silver in an ingot.

The fashion that the moneyer gives to the silver is then of the same kind as that given by the silversmith?

Precisely of the same kind.

What utility does the fashion of the moneyer give to the silver?

The impression on the money announces the weight and quality of the coin; that is, the quantity of fine metal and of alloy therein; consequently, it saves those who receive it the expence of weighing and assaying it.

Why do government reserve to themselves the exclusive right of coining money?

In order to prevent the abuses which individuals might create in this manufacture, by not making it of the same finenesss and weight which the impression indicates; and sometimes they reserve that right, in order to obtain the profit of it, which makes part of its revenue.

Cannot the government, by virtue of this exclusive privilege of coining money, raise the value of money much beyond the expences of manufacturing this merchandise?

It can do so, by reducing greatly the quantity of pieces coined, or the amount of the money.

What would happen then?

The money-merchandise becoming more scarce in proportion to the quantity of other merchandise in circulation, that is, which we are disposed to sell or to buy; this money-merchandise would be more in demand relatively to all other merchandise. We should give *less* money in exchange for *more* of other goods; in other words, goods would fall in price.

Should we not feel in commerce some inconvenience arising from the scarcity of money?

If that effect took place, the inconvenience would not be lasting, because the total *real* value of the money would not be diminished by it. There would be fewer pieces, but each of the pieces would be worth more; or, in other words, other goods would nominally fall in price, and their sum total would still bear exactly the same proportion with the sum total of the money.

What inconvenience would be felt in this case?

The ingots and utensils of gold and silver, being a different kind of merchandise from money, although made of the same material, would fall in price like all other merchandise: this would make a great disproportion between these metals in money and in ingots. There would be a considerable gain in converting them into money, which is an inducement to counterfeit and fabricate false money.

You have just shewn in what case money-merchandise rises in value with respect to other merchandise; in what case does it fall with respect to such merchandises?

When the quantity of the money is augmented relatively to all other merchandise, then *more* money is offered for *less* merchandise: the money would fall; in other words, the other merchandise would become *nominally* dearer.

You say nominally; but is it not really, when it is not the name of the money which is changed, and we actually give a greater weight of metal?

The value of the metal is, in this case, *really* less; but the value of the other merchandise, not having really changed, the variation of their price is only nominal. With the same quantity of corn, we purchase the same quantity of stuff. A bushel of corn, instead of being worth six shillings, is worth twelve; but a yard of cotton, instead of costing two shillings, costs four: thus, to buy three yards of stuff, we are still obliged to sell a bushel of corn as before; and a bushel of corn, though worth double the quantity of money, is still only equal to the value of the same quantity of stuff.

This is what happened when the discovery of the mines of South America threw into circulation an immense quantity of gold and silver, in comparison to what there had been before. To obtain the same quantity of corn, we must now give nearly three times as much silver as before the discovery of these mines.

America has then thrown into circulation three times as much silver as there was before?

She has circulated much more; but commerce, population, and riches, having greatly augmented since this discovery, the necessity for gold and silver, as well for the purposes of money as for furniture and ornaments, has greatly augmented also; and has prevented the precious metals from suffering a depreciation in proportion to their abudance. They have been produced in ten times the quantity, but have been three times more in demand.

What happens when, under the same denomination of money, a guinea, *for example, the government gives less metal than it gave before.*

The value of the money, which had fallen *really* with respect to other merchandise, then falls *nominally*.

Explain that by an example.

When the piece, called *six livres tournois*, does not contain more silver than that which was before called three livres tournois, we do not obtain for six livres more merchandise than we before obtained for three livres; that is, the same quantity of merchandise costs the same weight of silver. The value of the ingot of silver has scarcely varied from the year 1636 to the present time: with an ounce of silver we can buy the same quantity of those goods, whose value appears to have undergone the least variation. The *setier* of corn sold commonly for twelve livres tournois, and the same *setier* sold in 1789 for twenty-four livres; but twenty-four livres in 1789 did not contain a greater weight of silver, than in 1636 there was in twelve livres.*

What effect does this produce on the interests of individuals?

With respect to debts contracted previously by the government, if it pays them in money which is really worth less, it becomes bankrupt by all that there is less in the value of the new, than there had been in the old money.

And when it authorizes individuals to discharge their former debts in the new money, it authorizes them to commit a similar bankruptcy to its own.

With regard to the bargains made by individuals after the change in the money, this change produces no inconvenience; the bargains are made according to the real value of the new money.

Does a nation, whose money is carried into other countries, lose in consequence of this operation?

No, for the individuals who send it, take care to obtain at least an equal value in return.

Does the nation gain by such an exportation?

Yes, when she takes care not to coin money gratuitously, and never to manufacture this kind of merchandise, unless she is sufficiently indemnified for the employment of her capital and the wages of her industry.

What relation is there between the value of gold and silver?

Their relative values vary continually, and in different places, like the relative values of any other merchandise whatever. The value of the gold is raised in regard to that of silver, if gold is more demanded or less offered; hence the agio one is obliged sometimes to pay for the purchase of gold coin with silver money.

Does the same variation exist between copper and silver monies?

Not commonly; because we do not receive copper money pure, nor that of copper mixt with silver, which is called *billon*, at the rate of its intrinsic value, but in consequence of the facility which it affords for obtaining a piece of silver. If a hundred sous, which are paid me in copper, are intrinsically worth no more than four francs, what does it signify to me: I receive them for five francs, because I am sure to get for them, whenever I please, a piece of five francs. But when copper money becomes too abundant, and one can no longer obtain for it at pleasure the quantity of silver that it represents, its value is altered, and it can be no longer disposed of without loss.

Repeat to me summarily the essential principles which relate to money.

The numerous exchanges, and other transactions which cannot be dispensed with in a populous and civilized society, render absolutely necessary the use of an intermediate merchandize, which is money.

This merchandise is commonly of silver, manufactured for that purpose.

The value of this merchandise is established, like all other metals, in direct proportion to the demand for it, or of the necessity one has for it; and in inverse proportion to the quantity offered, or of the quantity which is actually in circulation.

The metal coined into money is a merchandise, totally different from the metal fashioned into any other thing. An ounce of metal in money may equal in value two ounces of metal in an ingot; because it is not in the power of every body to convert the ingot into money: but an ounce of metal in an ingot cannot be worth much more than an ounce of metal in money, because any body cannot convert the money into an ingot.

Whatever be the name given to any piece of money, whether it is called three lives or six livres, it is not really worth, as it regards other merchandise, more than the value of the metal and the fashion; but this fashion may be paid for too dearly, as it is exclusive, and as government keeps to itself the right of coining money.*

Notes

[*] The marc of silver, of the standard of the mint (of Paris), was worth about twenty-five livres in 1636; in 1789, fifty livres tournois. In England, where no alteration had been made in the weight or fineness of the money, scarcely any variation took place in the price of corn: the average of seven years previous to 1636, was about 6s. 1¾d. and for seven years previous to 1790, was 5s. 10¾d. per bushel. — Tr.

[*] It was not possible, in an elementary work like this, to include any but the most important principles, and which were essential to the interest of the public. The subject is treated at length in the Treatise on Political Economy.

CHAPTER XIX.
ON SIGNS REPRESENTING MONEY.

Why do you not call money a sign representative of merchandises?

Because it is no more a sign representative of merchandise, than any one merchandise is the sign of another. A cloth merchant might as well say, that the cloth in his warehouse is the sign which represents bread and meat, because, after an exchange or two, he might get bread and meat for his cloth.

What do you call signs representative of money?

Titles, documents, or vouchers, which have no intrinsic value, but which acquire one by the right which they give to a certain quantity of money; such as bills of exchange, bonds, bank notes, &c.

What do you observe respecting bills of exchange?

1. That they do not give the right to receive a sum of money till the end of a certain term, which diminishes their value by all the amount of the interest and of the risk which the bearer runs of not being paid when they become due. On this account they cannot be generally sold for the full amount that they give the right to receive. Commonly the *discount* on them is lost.

2. That they are sometimes payable abroad, and consequently in foreign money. In order to sell them, this foreign money must be valued in the national money: it is this valuation which is called the *course of exchange*. The exchange is at *par* when the quantity of fine gold or silver, paid for the purchase of a foreign bill of exchange, is precisely equal to the quantity of these metals, which the bill of exchange gives the right of receiving abroad.

What do you observe respecting bank notes?

That they circulate among the public for the entire value which they represent, when one is certain, by means of the note, to receive that value whenever one thinks proper.

What assurance has the public that the notes of a bank will be punctually paid?

A well administered bank never issues a note without receiving for it a value in exchange. This value is commonly money, or ingots, or bills of exchange. That part of the deposit, which is in money, is at all times ready to discharge them. That part which is in ingots requires only the time necessary to sell them. That part which is in bills of exchange only requires one to wait, at the worst, till they become due, before their value can be used to discharge the notes. So that, if the bills of exchange bear the names of many solvent persons, and if the times of payment are not at too great a distance, the bearers of the notes run no other risk than a trifling delay.

But if these bills of exchange are paid when due, by notes of the bank instead of money . . . . .

Then those notes are in fact discharged.

Bank notes can then supply the place of money?

Yes, to a certain point; but only in places where an office is constantly open to exchange them for money; for they are no longer worth the full sum of money, the instant they cease to be exchangeable for money at pleasure.

What is a paper money?

It is a title which give no right to any real reimbursement, but to which public authority attributes a certain value: a title which is received at that value in the payments which are made to the government, and which it authorizes individuals to give in payment for the discharge of engagements which they have contracted with each other.

What is it that keeps up the value of paper money?

Sometimes rigorous measures taken against those who refuse to sell for paper money; sometimes the uses to which the government admits it, such as the payment of taxes, and of debts previously contracted, sometimes, and almost always, it is the absence of all other money-merchandise, so that the public, who has nothing else to substitute for the ordinary use of money, is obliged to apply to it from the absolute necessity there is for this kind of merchandise. Often it is all these things united which gives any value to paper money. These means would even give it a very considerable value, if the facility which there is of multiplying it at will, did not always, sooner or later, bring it into disrepute.

One cannot then, by multiplying paper money, multiply at will the riches of a country?

No.

Explain to me why.

Because the paper money can only replace a part of the riches of a country, that part which consists of coin; and the money itself, were it even gold or silver, forms but a small part of the riches of any country when compared with the value of all the things in it; land, houses, furniture, buildings of every kind, merchandise, and even industrious talents.

You say, were it even gold or silver. It appears to me, that in augmenting the mass of money of gold or silver, the real riches of a country are increased.

The quantity of sales and purchases in a country, require a certain monetary value devoted to that circulation. When the quantity of money is increased, without being necessary for the circulation of a country, the real value of the money declines, whatever may be its nominal value: and losing in value as much as it increases in quantity, the total riches is no greater. If the quantity of silver money were to be doubled, we should be obliged to pay two ounces of silver for what we before bought for one ounce; consequently, two millions of *nominal* money in silver would not be of more value than one million was formerly.

It is the same with paper money. If the quantity of this money had been increased tenfold, we could not obtain with ten notes of an hundred pounds more than had been before obtained with one note. Whatever name is given to this sum, it can never have in the whole more than a certain value; and this value, truly effective, whatever may be the material of which the money is made, is always determined by the wants of the circulation, and the state of civilization, of riches and of industry, in a country.

CHAPTER XX.
ON MARKETS.

What do you mean by markets?

Before answering this question, I beg you to remark, that those who engage in production are seldom occupied with more than one product, or at most a small number of products. A tanner produces nothing but leather; a clothier, cloth; one merchant deals in wine, another imports foreign goods; one cultivator raises the vine, another corn, a third cattle.

What consequences do you draw from that?

That none of them can enjoy the greatest part of the various articles for which he has occasion, except by means of exchanging the greater part of his own productions for those which he desires to consume: so that the greater part of the consumptions of society take place only in consequence of an exchange.

But when we are able easily to exchange our own productions for those which we want, we are said to have found ready markets for our products.

On what does the ready sale of any particular article depend?

On the vivacity of the demand for it.

On what does the vivacity of the demand depend?

On two motives, which are—1st. The utility of the product, that is, the necessity the consumer has for it:—2d. The quantity of other products he is able to give in exchange.

I conceive the first motive. As to the second, it appears to me that it is the quantity of money that the buyer possesses, which induces him to buy or not.

That is also true: but the quantity of money which he has, depends on the quantity of product with which he has been able to buy this money.

Could he not obtain the money otherwise, than by having acquired it by products?

No.

If he had received the money from his tenants . . . . ?

His tenant had received it from the sale of part of the products to which the earth had contributed.

If he had received the interest of a capital lent —?

The undertaker who employed that capital had received the money which he paid, on the sale of a part of the products to which his capital had concurred.

If the purchaser had obtained this money by gift or inheritance —?

The giver, or he from whom the giver had obtained it, had it in exchange for some product.

In every case the money, with which any product is purchased, must have been produced by the sale of another product; and the purchase may be considered as an exchange in which the purchaser *gives* that which he has produced, (or that which another has produced for him), and in which he *receives* the thing bought.

What do you conclude from this?

That the more the purchasers produce, the more they have to purchase with, and that the productions of the one procure purchasers to the other.

It appears to me, that if the buyers only purchased by means of their products, they have generally more products than money to offer in payment.

Every producer asks for money in exchange for his products, only for the purpose of employing that money again immediately in the purchase of another product; for we do not consume money, and it is not sought after in ordinary cases to conceal it: thus, when a producer desires to exchange his product for money, he may be considered as already asking for the merchandise which he proposes to buy with this money. It is thus that the producers, though they have all of them the air of demanding money for their goods, do in reality demand merchandise for their merchandise.

Then the more merchandise there is produced, the more animated is the demand for merchandise?

Without doubt. It is for this reason that countries, which are but little civilized, present few markets, and those for products but little varied; while in populous, industrious, and productive districts, the sales are repeated and considerable.

It is not necessary then, in order that markets should be extended and multiplied, to look for them in foreign countries?

No; it is sufficient that other products should be multiplied in our own country.

What is it that multiplies foreign markets?

The riches of neighbouring nations, and the activity of their production.

What consequence do you draw from that?

That each of them is interested in the prosperity of his neighbour, and every nation in the prosperity of all others: for it is only those who produce much that can readily give you any thing in exchange for your products: or which comes to the same thing, that can give you the value of them in money.

What other consequence follows from this?

That riches are not exclusive: that, so far from that which another man, or another people gains, being a loss to you, their gains are favourable to you; that it is only necessary for you to produce, not that which they produce easier than you, but that which they cannot fail to demand from you by means of their products; and that wars, entered into for commerce, will appear so much the more senseless as we become better informed.

CHAPTER XXI.
ON REGULATIONS OR RESTRAINTS OF INDUSTRY.

What regulations are commonly made relating to industry?

The laws and regulations made by governments on this subject, have for their object either to determine on what products we may or may not employ ourselves; or to prescribe the manner in which the operations of industry shall be carried on.

What examples are there of the manner in which a government determines the nature of the products in which we may engage?

In agriculture, when it prohibits such or such or a culture, as tobacco, or when it gives extraordinary encouragement to other crops, such as corn.

In manufactures, when it favours certain manufactures, such as silks, and prohibits or restrains others, such as cottons.

In commerce, when it favours by treaties, communications with certain countries, and interdicts it with others; or when it gives privileges to trade in certain articles, and prohibits it in others.

What is the effect of such regulations?

To direct the efforts of industry towards productions less suitable to the wants of the nation, and less lucrative to their producers.

On what evidence do you suppose that the favoured productions are less suitable to the wants of the nation and less lucrative?

By this alone, that these productions are not sufficiently paid for to be able to support themselves without such encouragement.

In what way do governments interfere in the manner in which products ought to be created?

In manufactures, public authority sometimes prescribes the number of those who are to be employed in them, and the conditions they must comply with, as when it establishes corporations, freedoms, and companies: or when it fixes the material which must be employed, the number of threads which the warp and weft of a stuff must contain, and subjects them to particular marks. In commerce it sometimes prescribes the route by which the merchandize must pass, the port at which it must be landed, &c.

What is the object of corporations and freedoms?

It is to prevent incapable or inexpert workmen from deceiving the consumers by delivering to them an article of inferior quality to that which it represents.

In what cases are the precautions taken by government to prevent such abuses, really useful?

When the verification is impossible, or at least very difficult to the purchasers; as in the case of apothecaries' drugs. The care which a government takes to ascertain the capacity and honesty of apothecaries, and even of physicians, is then incontestibly useful. The same may be said of that control by which it puts a stamp on all articles of gold or silver.

What is the inconvenience of corporations and freedoms?

The establishing, in favor of producers united in corporations, of a monopoly, that is, the exclusive trade in what they produce; a monopoly of which the workmen on the one hand, and the consumers on the other, are the victims.

Why the workmen?

Because the corporation, in limiting the number of undertakers, and in subjecting them to certain formalities, limits the free competition of those who might employ the workmen.

But if the workmen on their parts agree together to demand certain wages?

It is then the workmen who form an unauthorized corporation just as prejudicial as those which are authorised.

How do corporations establish a monopoly against the consumers?

The production not being open to the competition of all producers without distinction, the products are not permitted to fall to the rate at which they might have been afforded by the charges of production; in which are comprised, as we know, the profits of the different producers.

What inconvenience arises from the profits being raised beyond what they would have been if left to free competition? These profits forming part of the income of the nation, is not the income augmented by this monopoly?

That which the producers gain beyond the rate of free competition, is an excess of price lost by the consumer at the same time that it is gained by the producer. It is not a value created, but displaced; it is a portion of riches which goes out of one purse into another, and which diminishes the general riches on the one hand, as much as it increases it on the other.

But this loss is trivial to the consumer, while it is of importance to the productor.

It is little on each individual purchase; but when repeated on all the articles we purchase, it becomes considerable at the end of the year; and the expenses of individuals being thus greater in proportion to their incomes, it is the same as if their incomes were less with respect to their consumption: they are poorer.

CHAPTER XXII.
ON IMPORTATIONS, DUTIES, AND PROHIBITIONS.

What does the word importation *signify?*

The purchasing abroad and introducing into a country foreign merchandise.

What do you mean by prohibitions?

Forbidding certain merchandize to be introduced into a country. Sometimes without prohibiting them entirely, they are made to pay duties on importation, which diminishes the quantity imported.

What results from an absolute prohibition?

An absolute prohibition forces the capital and industry which would have been devoted to this kind of commercial production, to apply itself to some production less advantageous.

Why less advantageous?

Because we should not engage in it but for the impossibility of directing our industry in the other mode. The prohibition would be superfluous, if the prohibited production* was not the most advantageous.

What happens when instead of an absolute prohibition a duty only is laid on the product imported?

The evil is then only partial, and consists in a dearness equal to the amount of the duty. The consumer pays for the product more than it is worth.

What does it signify if the consumer pays dearer for any thing, since the producer gains by it?

The producer does not profit by it; for what it sells for more goes in charges of production which are lost to every body; or in contributions consumed for the service of the state.

Why do you say that the charges of production are lost to every body? It appears to me that such of these charges as are composed of the profits paid to producers, are not charges lost, since the producers profit by them.

The producers are people who sell the service of their land, their capital and their industrious talents, whose gains are not the greater when all these services afford a product less abundant but dearer.

When any regulations render it necessary, in order to create a pound of sugar, to employ more of the services of the land, capital, and industry, the sugar is dearer without the producers being greater gainers. If they receive more values in payment, they have also furnished more values in services.

Do not the prohibitions and the duties, by compelling the creation of a product in the interior of a country, create the profits which are made in such a production?

It only causes the profits which would have been made on a commercial production, to be replaced by other profits, probably less lucrative, made on a manufactured production.

Is not that a good? Are not our capitals better employed in putting into activity our own national industry than that of foreigners?

Yes: but when we make the consumers, that is, the nation, pay dearer for certain products, simply to support a greater number of national producers, it is just as if a part of the nation was compelled to devote a portion of its income to maintain workshops of charity. Perhaps no population is truly desirable but that which industry left to itself can naturally support.

You have just considered the import duties in their influence on the income, on the riches of a nation, and you have proved that without augmenting the income of a nation, they cause it to pay dearer for the objects it consumes; which is equivalent to a real diminution of its income. But if the state is in want of these duties for the public expenses, are they more mischievous than — any other kind of impost?

No; they are an impost on commercial production which procures us products from without, as the land tax is an impost on the products which come to us from the earth; as the personal contribution and licences are imposts on the interior manufactures. The effect of all these imposts is to increase the price of all products without augmenting the income of those who consume them. They are all useful in providing for the public expenses from which the nation derives advantage; but they never encourage production, nor augment the income of a country.

However favourable the suppression of the taxes which bear on industry and consumers might be, would it not be attended with some danger?

Yes, when the suppression is sudden. The laws, and in general the whole legislation of a country, have long since induced the particular employment of certain capitals in the productions in which they are actually engaged, and from which they cannot be withdrawn without losing a great part, and sometimes nearly the whole, of their value. For example, if on the faith of security from laws which had for a long time prohibited cotton goods, the manufacturers had laid out large sums in machinery fit for the manufacture of cotton goods only, and if, by a new law, foreign cottons might all at once be introduced at a cheaper rate, this law, though in fact favourable to the income of a country, since it is enabled to procure the same products at less expense, would be unfavourable to capitals, because it would reduce to nothing the value of all the capitals actually engaged in the production of cotton goods.

Besides, a part of the capital engaged in any kind of production is composed of the talents of the persons employed in this production; for the advances which apprenticeships require are a capital, and this capital is lost from the moment that the apprenticeship becomes useless. A new apprenticeship is necessary; that is, a new capital must be laid out. The loss of this kind of capital is the more painful, as it falls on the working class, who, in general, are little able to bear it.

And even in those cases in which a change in the legislation does not cause a total loss of capital, it always produces some evil. A building, by its arrangement and its situation, is convenient for a certain kind of industry; it loses part of its advantages if its destination must be changed. The simple change of the habitudes, the dependencies, and the connexions of producers, exposes them to serious losses. It is only with great circumspection, that even the most desirable ameliorations ought to be introduced; otherwise we are in danger of overturning many fortunes, and destroying the happiness of many families.

Notes

[*] It must not be forgotten that, by the word *production*, we understand the action of *commercial* as well as of all other industry. Rice is to France or England, a product of commercial industry as much as wheat is a product of its agricultural industry.

CHAPTER XXIII.
ON EXPORTATION.

What does the word exportation *signify?*

It signifies the selling and sending the indigenous productions of a country to foreign countries.

Is it beneficial to a country to sell abroad its indigenous products?

No doubt it is, for that multiplies its affairs, and its lucrative relations, which are always beneficial; and also it procures in return merchandise which we may seek for in vain in our own country, or which would cost much more.

Does not a nation gain more by selling to strangers than to its own people?

No; an internal market, when it produces the same profits as an external one, is quite as valuable to the nation, and is a better sign of increasing prosperity than exportation itself. In fact, if your fellow countrymen buy your goods, it is a proof that they produce something with which they can pay for them.

When a stranger travels into another country and spends his money there, does not that country gain all the money he leaves behind?

The country gains in that case, the value of the money which it has received from the traveller less than the value of the things which have been delivered to him in exchange for his money: for the value of what is given to him is as real as the value of the money received. The expenditure of a stranger produces an effect similar to an exportation of merchandise which is paid for in money.

The profits made on this production are gained, and these profits are generally advantageous, because a traveller cannot dispute the prices of what is sold to him as rigorously as the foreign merchant who purchases the merchandise of a country.

Is it beneficial to expend money in order to attract foreigners?

What is spent with this view diminishes by so much the profit of the sales which are made to them; exactly as the premiums and rewards which are given to encourage exportation, are so much taken from the profits which result from it, and sometimes even exceed them.

Why do most nations and most governments (who act in this case agreeably to the desires of those nations) endeavour by every means to increase the quantity of merchandise which they export to strangers, and to limit the quantity of those which they purchase from them?

It is because they are unacquainted with the true source of riches.

What is, according to them, the source of riches?

The mines of gold and silver; and, as these are not in our country, they think that they cannot become rich without selling to foreigners merchandise of their own production, and compelling them to pay for them in the precious metals.

On what do they found this opinion?

On a merchant not gaining any thing on his merchandise until it is sent out of his warehouse, at which time he exchanges it for gold or silver money.

Why does a nation, in regard to other nations, differ from a merchant in regard to his customers?

A merchant, like a nation, sells his products only to repurchase others, which are either necessary for his consumption or fit for the continuation of his commerce. But a merchant does not find in his customer, precisely the man who can furnish him with the goods or materials which he wants, and at the most advantageous price. It is only with the money of the buyer that he can himself buy what he wants, and in the quantities that are convenient to him.

It is not the same between one nation and another. The merchants, who are the agents of this communication, by the variety and the facility of their operations, are enabled to bring back in return for what they send out, merchandise which, if not useful to the dealer, whose products they have exported, will at least be so to some other. The last, in paying for it, will provide the means of paying the first.

The interest of merchants in all these operations, is to obtain in return such merchandise as is most in demand, because it will sell the best.

Would it not still be better that a neighbouring nation should pay us in money rather than in goods?

You do not desire this money, but in order to use it in the purchase of goods of which you are in want.

That is true; but when I have the money I am at liberty to employ it in the purchase of whatever I think proper.

A foreign nation who pays you in merchandise, gives you only such merchandise as you are willing to receive, for you are at liberty to purchase in return whatever you please.

But when she pays us in merchandise, this merchandise is consumed, and we lose the value of it; a loss which we should not have made if she had paid us in money.

The loss you make does not come from the importation, but from the consumption, of the merchandise. If at the close of an *external* commercial operation there is a value consumed under the form of *champaign*, the loss is not greater than when at the close of an *internal* commercial operation, the same value had been consumed in *cyder*.

The cyder would at least have been a product of the national industry.

The foreign goods are equally products of the national industry, since they are products of its commerce.

How does foreign commerce procure new values, new riches, since we must always give to foreigners a merchandise of equal value to that which they give to us?

An example will make you understand this. A merchant sends stuffs to Brazil; he obtains in that country, in exchange for his stuffs, a greater value than he gave for them in Europe, because they have gained by the carriage. This value which he has gained, he there exchanges for cotton which he brings back to Europe, the value of which is also augmented by the carriage. When these operations are finished, although the merchant has exchanged, in each place, his merchandise at the current price; that is, value for value; still as the value of the different products have increased while they were in his hands, he has, without robbing the stranger of any value, brought back to his own country a value superior to that which he had exported; which is equivalent to a value created in the country.

Every augmentation of riches, even in external commerce, is then the fruit of an internal production?

Yes, with the exception of plunder, in exchange for which nothing is given. But besides spoliation being criminal, because it is contrary to justice, it is odious, and consequently dangerous, and the advantages which it procures are uncertain, temporary, and scarcely ever profitable.

Why do you say, scarcely ever profitable?

Because when we seize upon goods created by others, we rob them at the same time of the means of continuing to create new ones, and we can only enjoy them for once, as when we cut down a tree to get at its fruit. The goods thus obtained are besides of very little profit, because they are seldom obtained when wanted, or when they could be made a good use of, but must be taken when they can be got. They may be carried off; but the carriage itself constitutes a great part, and sometimes the whole of their value. They are consumed; and generally the greater part of them, on the spot; they are wasted rather than used, and their consumption often creates more evil than good.

CHAPTER XXIV.
ON POPULATION.

What are the causes which increase or diminish the population of a country?

In general a country is so much the more populous as it produces more values or riches for the maintenance of its inhabitants, and so much the less so as it produces less riches.

Why do not you say more of the commodities proper for the food of men?

Because there are commodities which, without being alimentary, are necessary to life, as clothes and lodging, and because with those which are not alimentary we can procure, by means of commerce and exchange, those which are. It is sufficient for a country to produce values to enable it to exist; the nature of the values will immediately accommodate itself to its wants; for the commodities of which it stands in the greatest need, are those for which it will pay best, and the good price they will then obtain will cause them to become abundant.

But when war or bad laws prevent the arrival of articles of the first necessity, such as those which serve for subsistence, will not the population suffer greatly?

It will suffer the same as when crops fail in bad years.

Without supposing any scourge on the part of men or of nature, if the number of births exceeds what the products of a nation can nourish, what will be the consequence?

It will necessarily follow that part of those born, will perish of want, either in childhood or at a riper age. This evil exists at all times, more or less, because the human species, like all other organised beings, has more means of increase than it has of maintenance. Want does not instantly kill, but it gradually wastes. Few people die for want of food, but for want of food sufficiently abundant or sufficiently wholesome; for want of medicine in illness, for want of cleanliness, for want of rest, for want of dry and warm lodging, and for want of those attentions which we cannot do without in infirmity and old age. From the moment that any one of these objects becomes necessary to them, and they cannot obtain it, they languish for a greater or a less period, and sink at the first shock.

Who first feel the want of the necessaries of life?

The scarcity of one or other of these means of existence, first raises the price of it; it thus gets out of the reach, first of the most indigent; and as the scarcity and dearness increases, the greater is the number of those who suffer from its privation.

Do not wars, epidemics, and in general those plagues which cut off great numbers of men, enable those which are left to enjoy a greater quantity of those commodities of which they are in want?

These scourges, in destroying men, destroy at the same time the means of production; and we do not see that, in countries thinly populated, the wants of the inhabitants are more easily satisfied. It is the abundance of productions, and not the scarcity of consumers, which procures a plentiful supply of whatever our necessities require; and the most populous countries are in general the best supplied.

What is it that induces men to assemble together in villages, towns, or cities?

The nature of their occupations. Those who cultivate the earth spread themselves all over the country, in order to be near their employment, and to have a small distance to carry their crops at harvest time. Those who carry on manufactories place themselves in towns, where they find at hand the materials, utensils, and the artisans of which they are frequently in want. Those who engage in commerce place themselves either in the sea-ports, where the merchandise arrives more easily, or on the roads by which it is distributed through various provinces or countries. Those who produce by means of their lands, but without cultivating them; or by means of their capital, without employing them themselves, being able to expend their incomes in any place whatever, live where they please, but generally in cities, where they find greater resources and amusements of every kind. It is the same with those whose profits are founded on immaterial products; which, not being transportable, are therefore consumed chiefly in places where a number of persons are collected together. It is for this reason that we meet with so many physicians, advocates, and public functionaries in great cities.

Are not great cities a burden to a nation, since they must be provisioned by the country?

By no means: for the inhabitants of cities have incomes equally real with the inhabitants of the country. They do not live at the expense of the latter, as they do not receive from them any value without giving them another value in exchange. And the country cannot have markets more certain or more extensive than the cities, to which they present in their turn, when well cultivated and they are able to purchase much, important markets for the products of manufacture and commerce. Thus there is not a more certain indication of the riches and great revenues of a country, than numerous and extensive cities.

CHAPTER XXV.
ON COLONIES.

What do you mean by Colonies?

Establishments which the inhabitants of one country form in another land, in order to live there more at ease.

Are there different kinds of colonies?

They may either be dependent or independent of the metropolis. The metropolis is the nation from which the colony went forth.

What do you mean by colonies dependent on the metropolis or mother country?

I understand those which are subject to the same government, and governed by laws which it imposes on them.

What effect has this dependence on the relative riches of the colonies and the metropolis?

That the metropolis can compel the colony to purchase from her every thing it may have occasion for; that this monopoly, or this exclusive privilege, enables the producers of the metropolis to make the colonists pay more for the merchandise than it is worth.

The metropolis, then, gains more from the colony than if she was independent?

Yes; but all that the tradesmen and merchants of the metropolis sell too dear, is paid for too dear by the colonial consumers. It is a value which has gone from the purse of one individual to that of another, both citizens or subjects of the same country. These values appear a great deal in the hands of those who gain them, because they are but few; and small to those who pay them, because they are divided amongst many individuals: but the loss is not the less to the colony, which is so much the poorer by it.

Are not the colonies indemnified in some other manner for the usurious gains which are made from them?

They make in their turn an usurious gain on the consumptions of the metropolis, which is not permitted to purchase from any other than them, the colonial products of which they are in want. On the one side and on the other it is a combination, or conspiracy of the producers against the consumers.

Are there any other inconveniencies attending independent colonies?

Their administration is corrupt and expensive, because it is superintended from too great a distance: and the metropolis is obliged to keep up garrisons, and military and naval forces, either to enable it to hold, or to defend them. And these expences increase the burthens, either of the people of the colony, or of those of the metropolis, without taking into account the wars which are always brought on by such an order of things.

Do these evils take place when the colonies are independent?

Never. They establish a government for themselves which costs them very little; they are no expence to the metropolis; and the one and the other, the metropolis and the colony, enjoy the advantages which two civilized nations derive from their reciprocal communications.